Bono
The Biography

Bono
The Biography

Laura Jackson

PIATKUS

Copyright © 2001 by Laura Jackson

First published in 2001 by
Judy Piatkus (Publishers) Limited
5 Windmill Street
London W1T 2JA
e-mail: info@piatkus.co.uk

Reprinted 2001 (twice)

The moral right of the author has been asserted

A catalogue record for this book is available from the British Library

ISBN 0 7499 2245 1

Text design Paul Saunders
Edited by Kelly Davis

This book has been printed on paper manufactured with respect for the
environment using wood from managed sustainable resources

Typeset by Action Publishing Technology, Gloucester
Printed and bound in Great Britain by Butler & Tanner Ltd, Frome, Somerset

Dedicated to my husband David
– a quite extraordinary gem of a man

I have great admiration for Bono,
both personally, and for his dedication
to campaigning to end the crushing burden
of Third World debt. Through his stature
in the worlds of music and entertainment,
Bono has educated and inspired thousands
of individuals, especially young people,
to become involved in this vital political issue.
He is a genuine friend of the United Nations,
and has made a real difference to the
lives of the world's poor.

United Nations Secretary-General Kofi Annan
March 2001

Contents

Acknowledgements

Grateful appreciation to everyone whom I interviewed. My thanks for all contributions to: Janine Allis-Smith; United Nations Secretary-General Kofi Annan; Sue Darcy; Jamie Drummond; Garret Fitzgerald; Martin Forwood; Scott Gorham; Archbishop Desmond Tutu.

Thanks also to: Births, Deaths and Marriages, Dublin; Central Library, Dublin (Kitty McDonnell); Elgin Library staff; *Irish Independent*; *Irish Times*; Shashi Tharoor, Director of Communications and Special Projects, United Nations, New York; Lavinia Browne, Reconciliation Commission, Cape Town; Nigel Monckton, Press Officer, Sellafield, Cumbria; SDLP Headquarters, Belfast (Gemma); Greenpeace, London (Ruby Maguire and Pete Myers); *Hot Press*; *Sunday Tribune*; *Sun*; *Q* magazine; CORE, Barrow-in-Furness.

Special thanks to: David, for his invaluable help as ever with research; and to Katie Andrews and all staff at Piatkus Books, London.

CHAPTER 1

Firebrand

O N 24 MARCH 2001 at the National Car Rental Center, Fort Lauderdale, in Miami, Florida, U2 kickstarted the Elevation Tour, their first return to the road in three years. From the moment the tour had been announced, anticipation had run high among the supergroup's global legions of loyal fans.

For over two decades the veteran Irish rockers have had a pathological resistance to standing still. Creatively curious, they have continued to experiment fearlessly – albeit, on occasions, with mixed results. Characteristically unpredictable, this time they offered a ruthlessly stripped-down presentation – in stark contrast to the flashy techno extravaganza of their Zoo TV and Pop Mart outings in the 1990s.

They could afford to be supremely confident, for their tenth studio album *All That You Can't Leave Behind* had effortlessly matched the instant UK chart-topping success of their latest single, 'Beautiful Day'. In addition to selling over five million copies in it's first few weeks on sale, the album had gone to the top in a total of thirty-two countries. Even after so long a break, and amid the glut of heavily promoted new teenage music stars, U2 were clearly still at the top of their game.

No one would claim that the members of U2 began in 1976 as virtuoso musicians, but certainly it was a shared interest in music that drew them together. At the hub of this vibrant four-piece band – comprising bass player Adam Clayton, lead guitarist David Evans (universally known as the Edge) and drummer Larry Mullen – is the 41-year-old Dublin-born singer/songwriter Bono. Over the years, he has been as much a lightning rod for critical acclaim as a subject for cutting caricature.

His elevation to – at times Messianic – rock icon status would have been hard to predict when he was a child. A faint ambition to become an actor had briefly flared and died. And neither was Bono a natural songbird, desperate for the chance to flex his vocal cords. Indeed, of singing he would later confess, 'It's something I never really thought of that much.' Yet he was a born communicator, with a flair for the dramatic, who loved to draw attention to himself.

He remembers his formative years as having been largely spent learning to look after himself in Dublin's rough streets. Though never a rebel, he acquired the lurid nickname of 'The Antichrist'. This was a strange sobriquet for a charismatic, if intense, youth who, in his mid-teens, became a member of his school's Christian Union. As the son of parents from either side of the religious divide, he also grew up to be a rampant inclusionist with a deep intolerance of bigotry, whose first musical inspiration came from psalms and hymns.

Throughout his life Bono has been a mass of contradictions. Just one of the signs of his inner complexity to emerge in adulthood would be his creation of bizarre alter-egos: a motley cast of disturbing stage characters who included the wildly egotistical The Fly, the gaudy Mirrorball Man and the devilishly seedy MacPhisto.

Habitually clad in black, with his trademark wraparound dark glasses, Bono is a distinctive and enduring figure in the ephemeral world of pop. But, in addition to ranking among the top echelon of rock's most important frontmen, the politically savvy superstar is also renowned as a committed pacifist and a tireless crusader for human rights.

He is as much at home on stage energizing tens of thousands of delirious fans, as he is partying at the White House Millennium bash, or lobbying support for the world's poorest nations at the US Senate. Yet this is all a far cry from the singer's less exalted beginnings.

Bono's real name is Paul David Hewson and he was born on 10 May 1960 in the Rotunda Hospital in Dublin, in the Republic of Ireland, the second son of Iris Elizabeth Hewson and Brendan Robert Hewson (known as Bobby Hewson), a Post Office worker.

When his parents took the dark-haired infant with blue-grey eyes home to meet his seven-year-old brother Norman, it was to 36 Dale Road. The family subsequently moved to 10 Cedarwood Road, Ballymun, a two-storey, semi-detached house with a sizeable front garden in the north side of the capital where Paul had a lower middle-class upbringing.

His education began at Dublin's Glasnevin National Primary School, from where, in summer 1971, he progressed to St Patrick's Secondary School for Boys. By the following academic year, however, he had moved again. This time he went to the city's Mount Temple High School, Ireland's first inter-denominational, co-educational comprehensive school.

Bono's enrolment in this controversial mould-breaking establishment was entirely in keeping with his parents' sometimes unconventional attitudes. Iris Rankin and Bobby Hewson had both hailed from the centre of Dublin; indeed, they had grown up on the same street, Oxmantown Road. She was Protestant, while he was Roman Catholic. But they refused to allow the intense rivalry in Ireland between these religions to keep them apart. Bravely, they married – in the teeth of intense opposition.

Moreover, although tradition dictated that children of a mixed marriage be raised in the Catholic faith, the couple instead opted to bring up their sons as Protestants. Consequently, every Sunday, Bono's father would attend Mass in Finglas, then wait outside the nearby Church of Ireland church where his wife and children worshipped. This segregation would inflame Bono and laid the foundations for his views on the need to pursue integration and greater tolerance of different faiths.

Religious teachings and trappings, in one sense or another, played a prominent role in the growing boy's life. He possessed an intensely acute way of thinking. And the trials and tribulations endured by the Biblical David on his odyssey to becoming the king of Israel gripped the twelve-year-old's vivid imagination. He was inspired by his surroundings in church, fascinated by the stories played out in the colourful, ornate stained-glass windows.

Musically, too, the future rock star is adamant that the uplifting words and music that reverberated around the vaulted stone ceiling of the church spoke more loudly to him than any fire and brimstone-style sermon could have. They also touched an, as yet unrecognized, artistic nerve. He later declared that, to him, the psalms were often akin to blues music.

But the stimulation did not always have the expected result. The older he got, the more he questioned all the religious dogma, until he started to rebel. He once explained, 'In Ireland, they force-feed you religion to the point where you throw it up.' He disliked the unbending constraints that were inherent in both his parents' religions – so much so that he began to see religion itself as 'the perversion of faith'.

Certain aspects of his own identity were also starting to confuse him at this time. 'When I was growing up, I didn't know where I came from,' he has admitted. That confusion related specifically to whether he ought to consider himself as middle class or working class.

He lived in a comfortable, spacious enough house, very different from the cramped, high-rise problem-laden, then notorious, tower blocks most closely associated with a Ballymun address. But as to whether to class himself as Protestant or Catholic, he later revealed, 'I always felt like I was sitting on the fence.'

At least the non-denominational Mount Temple High School provided Bono with a freer, more relaxed environment in which to breathe as he studied. Having been something of a daydreamer at primary school, he would not, overall, prove to be an exceptional scholar, but he did find an aptitude for certain subjects, including history and art.

Yet there was always so much more filling Bono's head and heart. His personality seemed to have two co-existing, often conflicting, sides. From a young age he was a lively, inquisitive extrovert who had the gift of the gab. He exhibited an infectious, sometimes overwhelming, enthusiasm and an unquenchable thirst for knowledge. He also enjoyed involvement with people, clubs and associations and was becoming quite a romantic at times.

At the same time, he could be decidedly headstrong, and challenging to the point of being argumentative. Given to moody spells that rendered him unpredictable, even aggressive, some of those around him jokingly began to call him 'the Antichrist'. For a while the nickname stuck.

The sibling rivalry common in many families can go deeper still between two brothers with a big age difference. In this case, though, Bono unhesitatingly takes the lion's share of the blame for the frequent fights that erupted between himself and Norman. He once made the sad claim that he had no nice childhood memories and that was before the bombshell that exploded on the family in the autumn of 1974.

Whilst attending her father's funeral, Iris Hewson suddenly collapsed. Four days later, on 10 September, she died of a brain haemorrhage. Bono was fourteen. He later stated bluntly that he had not enjoyed a particularly close relationship with his parents up to that point. But when Iris died, he felt cheated of the chance of ever forging a close bond with his mother.

Norman Hewson, now in his early twenties, had by 1974 already left home, which left Bono alone with his father. There ensued a couple of very bumpy years for them both. Bono has often declared that one direct consequence of his mother's untimely death was to change where he lived from being a home into merely a house.

Anger propelled Bono through much of his adolescence – anger at the rigidity of religion, anger at capitalist greed. Showing early environmentalist leanings, he felt tangible rage when a nearby building development came at the cost of mature lush woodland. And added to this was the running sore of resentment at having been robbed of maternal affection by his mother's unexpected death. It all amounted to a harsh and unforgiving barrier being erected around the teenager – a barrier that was compounded by a lack of easy communication between himself and his father.

In fact, it was Bobby Hewson who held the family together through these testing years. But Bono would be much older before he could properly appreciate that. Looking back, he candidly acknowledged the extent of his difficult behaviour when he described himself as having been a, 'sixteen-year-old rentabastard'.

Nevertheless, although street life in his neck of the woods some-times meant street fights, Bono has insisted that he never instigated trouble. On the other hand, he was certainly not a turn-the-other-cheek kind of guy.

Defensive involvement was occasionally necessary if only to avoid having his head split open. On those occasions when he did get involved, however, he usually emerged as the victor. But, far from revelling in such behaviour, it often preyed on his mind after-wards and made him wary of possible future repercussions.

It seems strange then that this firebrand, with his unconven-tional views on religion, should suddenly, around the age of fifteen, join his school's Christian Union. But spiritual faith was, and remains, very important to Bono.

On an earthier plane, girls, by now, had also become very impor-tant to the teenager. Though not tall and with a compact, sturdy build, Bono drew on his clear blue-eyed good looks, his cheeky smile and his attractively assertive personality to win over the girls, whom he became a dab hand at romancing.

His other interests, meantime, were beginning to take shape. Possibly sparked by his father's occasional appearance in local amateur theatre productions, Bono nursed an intense, if short-lived, desire to become an actor. But that ambition withered away when he discovered that Dublin had no acting school. Taking part in some school drama classes was as far as he got.

But there were other ways of performing on stage, and music began to beckon. From the inspirational psalms and hymns to which he'd first been attracted, Bono's interest in music had traversed traditional Irish folk music before focusing on glam rock which dominated the mid-1970s British pop scene. Its showmanship and imagery appealed to him.

Years earlier, his brother Norman had introduced him to the guitar but Bono had merely tinkered with the instrument and had never progressed beyond the proverbial three chords. Nor had he, so far, considered himself to be a singer. So it was odd that in 1976 he should respond to a small note pinned to the noticeboard at school – an appeal to recruit any like-minded soul who was interested in forming a rock band.

Bono may have had to be persuaded by a friend to go along and answer the call, but in good old rock 'n' roll tradition it was a decision that would irrevocably change his life.

CHAPTER 2

Believer

THE CALL TO ARMS had been placed on Mount Temple High School's bulletin board by fellow Dubliner, Larry Mullen. Born Laurence Joseph Mullen on 31 October 1961 in the city's Artane district, the blond-haired, blue-eyed son of a civil servant had been taught to play piano but had been drawn to the drums with dreams of forming a rock band. In summer 1976, Mullen, not yet fifteen, had invited hopefuls along to the family home at 60 Rosemount Avenue in the northside and several students had responded.

They included bass player Adam Charles Clayton. Born on 13 March 1960 in Chinnor, Oxon, with his cherubic blond curls and blue eyes, Adam was just a child when, due to his father's job as an airline pilot, his family had left England to live abroad before eventually settling in Dublin.

The two brothers who also showed up that day – David Howell Evans and Dick Evans – likewise originally hailed from Britain. It had been a year after David's birth in East London on 8 August 1961 that the Evans family had gone to make a new life in the Emerald Isle, settling into the middle-class Dublin suburb of Malahide. Like Larry Mullen, David Evans had taken piano lessons but both he and brother Dick had quickly turned to the guitar.

As the day progressed it was clear that the would-be band was top-heavy with guitarists. To add to Mullen's drum kit, the Evans brothers and Clayton between them could bring one bass guitar, one acoustic guitar and one electric guitar, plus two amplifiers. On the face of it, it was hard to see what Bono, who had likewise made his way to Rosemount Avenue, had to offer.

In fact, Bono did not exhibit any particularly outstanding musical talent at that first gathering, despite harbouring aspirations to become the band's lead guitarist. But he did exude an irresistible verve and optimism, as well as a confident theatrical flair, and that made him a natural choice as frontman and, therefore, lead singer.

At this point Bono was a hyped-up sixteen-year-old, who could barely talk fast enough to keep up with his own enthusiasms. Larry Mullen may have been the prime mover behind the band's formation, but he would later admit that he was in charge for all of five minutes – until Bono arrived. One or two others straggled into the Mullen family kitchen that Saturday afternoon but the band formed with these five.

With the demise, early in the decade, of progressive rock (a genre which had featured the elite musicianship of bands like Wishbone Ash), popular music had passed through the mellowing fun phase of glam rock, from which it was just emerging. And frankly, it was fortunate timing for Bono and company because the 'qualifications' for forming a band now placed less emphasis on musical ability, and more on exhibiting enough raw enthusiasm to project an attitude.

Raring to go, the boys immediately started meeting for rehearsals, usually at school or in the garden shed at the Evans' family home. There they would hole up for hours, practising – manfully making the best of their cheap underpowered equipment. Tellingly, however, it was the shattering feedback frequently heard screeching from one of their dodgy amps that gave rise to the band's first name.

As Feedback, the five-piece schoolboy band performed the

standard cover versions of sixties classics and some lighter-weight, current hits. But this type of music was not their forté, and when they tried out their skills in front of live audiences they suffered more than their fair share of hecklers.

Bono had derived his earliest musical inspiration from listening to the Beatles, the Rolling Stones and the Beach Boys. He liked David Bowie, and he had also responded strongly to the androgynous appeal of Marc Bolan, singer with the glam band T Rex – a fact that had surprised him. 'I'm not gay,' Bono later said. 'That was just the pure power of the music.'

Lately, though, he had begun to feel that the music world was on the cusp of a new era. Within the band they were excitedly anticipating just such a prospect when, in November 1976, the single 'Anarchy in the UK' by the Sex Pistols erupted onto the scene.

The aggressive, in-your-face nihilism of punk rock was a shock to the system for many but Bono saw the radical, influential – if short-lived – movement as an intriguing expression of individuality. Never shy of drawing attention to himself, he promptly became the first punk rocker at Mount Temple High School. Outraging teachers and astonishing fellow pupils by attending classes dressed garishly, with savagely shorn hair and the requisite chain slung across one side of his face from nose to ear, he enjoyed the controversy he aroused.

Feedback introduced 'Anarchy in the UK' into their repertoire but they were still struggling. Certainly they performed with plenty of heart, but Bono's early attempts to earnestly connect with audiences were totally unappreciated. David Evans later bluntly admitted, 'We were the worst cover version band in the world.'

Yet, far from deflating the band, this experience instead made them realize that their salvation lay in writing original material. The alluring prospect of performing their own compositions seized hold of their collective imagination. Ultimately each member would be involved in the development of songs, but it was Bono who became the band's major lyricist.

He began tentatively enough, scribbling away at ideas during quiet spells whilst working as a part-time petrol pump attendant. But he had found a niche, and discovering his creative potential – that fragile process in writing when an idea fills the void and crystallizes into something worthwhile – thrilled Bono.

He drew inspiration from the American rock star Bruce Springsteen, whom Bono later dubbed 'the Buddha of my youth'. Springsteen's ability to retain his independence and integrity within the ego-driven, bombastic music business, whilst writing meaningful songs, was something Bono greatly admired.

From the outset, his lyrics expressed the deepest aspects of his personality, and reflected his concern over life and death issues and the world as he saw it. The many sides of his nature would fuse often in the coming years, making Bono a passionate, socially aware songwriter with his own immense power to inspire. For now, though, he had to feel his way forward.

Life at this juncture was a mixed picture. Bono was still not especially close to his father; though, as the singer has himself admitted, he was not an easy youth to live with. The opera-loving Bobby Hewson was, like most parents, on a different plane from his teenage son. He also emerged as a man who, by nature, was economic with his praise.

Most importantly, Bono had about him a pervading sense of rootlessness. This stemmed partly from the continuing belief that his was a house, rather than a home, and partly from his own nomadic spirit. He recognized in himself an inherent wanderlust – he could always happily kip down for the night on a mate's floor, instead of returning to 10 Cedarwood Road. On the other hand, he did have some real anchors in his life. These came from his involvement with the band and from maintaining his spiritual faith through the Christian Union and the church.

Outside school, Bono had also joined an association called Lypton Village. This group of teenagers shared an unconventional outlook on life. They included two friends of Bono's called Derek Rowan (nicknamed Guggi) and Gavin Friday (whose real name is Fionan Hanvey). Both were singers with the Virgin Prunes, a local performance art band that would become most noted for its outrageous transvestite stage image.

Members of Lypton Village often congregated at Gavin Friday's house to listen to music and to engage in lively and convoluted discussions. It was a fertile breeding ground for creative ideas, and Bono welcomed these stimulating encounters. Lypton Village members also formed a ready-made travelling support unit for Feedback.

On the romance front, the charismatic, bold, yet curiously vulnerable, Bono had until now enjoyed playing the field. But for a long time he had had his sights firmly set on one particular girl at school, a dark-haired, very pretty, bright student called Alison Stewart who, at the same age as he, also came from Dublin's northside.

The snag was, Ali (as she is known) was also a strong-willed, independent character who had knocked Bono back at his first attempt to chat her up. Undaunted, he had spent years pursuing her, relying on his quick sense of humour to weaken her defences and eventually he won her over.

Ali, though, was determined to dictate the pace. Given Bono's footloose reputation, she had no intention of rushing headlong into a full-on relationship that might not last. That said, it was she who turned Bono into a one-woman man and, even this early, her more organized approach to life provided a much-needed touchstone for the volatile seventeen-year-old.

In many ways 1977 was a time of change. Lypton Village members were all given alternative names and Guggi ordained that Paul Hewson should be called Bono Vox – somewhat obscurely after an advertisement for a hearing aid retailer on Dublin's O'Connell Street. It took a bit of getting used to, and it is said that Bono initially disliked the nickname intensely. At any rate, the Vox would later be dropped.

Equally bizarrely, Bono then re-christened guitarist David Evans 'the Edge'. This is sometimes said to have had something to do with the shape of his skull. Another explanation was that the softly spoken young man had a tendency to stand back from the melée and observe goings-on from the periphery. More prosaically, it is also said to have been lifted from a notice for a local hardware shop. Whatever its true origins, this moniker also stuck.

The third name change came about when the band dumped Feedback in favour of calling themselves the Hype – a somewhat ambitious title for a band that had yet to make an impression.

For all that, their shared obsession with music, and the sheer white heat of ambition, continued to hold together a set of four very different personalities, individuals who would otherwise probably never have linked up as friends. But it worked.

Inevitably, there was a degree of natural competitiveness, some posturing and jockeying for position. But any tension this caused was counteracted by the strength of their friendship.

Early on, Bono recognized an odd unity between the four. With his tendency to romanticize, he saw them as renegades banding together outside the system. As rehearsals filled much of their free time, their friendship steadily developed.

Despite Bono's overpowering personality, the Hype remained pretty democratic. That said, Bono later called himself 'the mechanic of the band', and admitted to plaguing the others with endless demands to listen to and analyse records.

When it came to their own performance, originally a deal of bluff had been involved. But a characteristic sound was now developing. Adam Clayton's highly individual sense of rhythm gave their music a unique texture, accentuated by the unique sounds extracted from their respective instruments by the Edge and Larry Mullen. Nevertheless, it was a steep learning curve for them all.

Their sense of purpose was strengthened by their friends, on whom the band frequently tried out their latest material. On such occasions Bono could see, in their reaction, confirmation of his hopes. He recalled, 'The songs really did have a spark, that ability to affect people.'

Gig-wise, however, the five-piece Hype existed in hand-to-mouth fashion. They also relied heavily on the goodwill of some of their relatives for getting transport to gigs. In January 1978, in an enterprising attempt to improve their fortunes, the bass player tried a harmless bluff by placing an advert in a local newspaper which read: 'Manager seeks the whereabouts of the Hype after amazing Howth gig. It was great, lads.' The advert provided a name and telephone number.

Wherever they were headed, they were clearly going under their own steam – until, with the experience they'd gained playing in local pubs and clubs, including the Baggot Inn and Moran's, they had the confidence to enter a competition. This was to be their first breakthrough.

It was a talent contest, co-sponsored by the *Evening Press*, Harp Lager and CBS, held on 18 March 1978. One of the judges was CBS Records' A & R executive Jackie Hayden. They were up against experienced musicians and Bono was as conscious as the others that Hype's performance could be shaky. However, on the night, energized by an especially electric atmosphere, they had a real spark and it shone brightly enough to carry the day.

On top of the £500 prize money, their performance also persuaded an impressed Jackie Hayden to offer them studio time to record a demo. Within weeks the band found themselves in Keystone Studios. Unfortunately, but perhaps understandably given their inexperience, it turned out to be something of a rushed and unrewarding affair. The session was certainly useful experience, but it did little else for the band.

By now the band was minus one man. After the talent contest Dick Evans had decided to quit. The Edge's elder brother wanted to go to Dublin's Trinity College to study engineering. He played one further gig at Howth Community Centre before bailing out; although he would, in time, return to music, joining the Virgin Prunes.

After Dick Evans' departure, the band changed their name for the third and final time. From now on, they were to be known as U2. The suggestion came from an acquaintance of theirs, Steve Averill. Using the stage name Steve Rapid, he was the lead singer with local punk rock band the Radiators.

U-2 was the name of a particular type of Lockheed Reconnaisance aeroplane. In May 1960 a thirty-year-old US civilian pilot named Francis Gary Powers had been detected violating Soviet air space in just such a plane. Powers maintained that he had unwittingly strayed off-course while carrying out weather research. The Russians called it a spying mission and shot the aircraft down. This event created a serious international incident and damaged an already tense American-Soviet relationship.

Apart from the fact that this furore had hogged the headlines around the time Bono was born, it's hard to know quite why the band chose this as their name. For whatever reason, they liked the suggestion. It was also unique-sounding, and to Bono the inclusionist overtones of U2 dovetailed neatly with his ambition for the band's appeal to cross all barriers.

But, at this stage, reaching out to vast audiences was still a distant dream. Then, in early April, before their Keystone Studios sessions, they met Bill Graham, a journalist with the Irish rock magazine *Hot Press*, who would become an influential ally and a good friend.

Bono credits Adam Clayton with having been a tireless dynamo when trying to get the band attention. Certainly, the bass player constantly harassed Bill Graham to come and hear them play – even relentlessly ringing the journalist at home. Eventually these tactics produced the man in person. (Graham was normally wary of what he called the 'doubtful merits of Irish music competitions'. Merely winning the talent contest in itself would not have been enough to make him put in a personal appearance.)

They met one Saturday afternoon in a pub near Mount Temple High School and Bill Graham was impressed by the four-man unit's intense focus and curiosity. At the same time, he registered just how open to advice they were. He had also been particularly struck by Bono's energy and his candour.

The immediate upshot of the meeting was the first of U2's many interviews for *Hot Press* which appeared in the 28 April 1978 edition. They were described as a promising new Dublin four-piece. But Bill Graham's impact had only just begun, for in less than a month he put them in touch with a friend of his, Paul McGuinness, a businessman who already managed several bands including the Stranglers.

After attending a U2 gig at Dublin's Project Arts Centre on 25 May, Paul McGuinness added U2 to his stable. McGuinness had been impressed by the whole band's demeanour. He also later singled out Bono, this time because of his unusual insistence on making determined, almost defiant, eye contact with the audience.

Things were getting interesting. In spring 1978 Bono had returned to sit a further final year at Mount Temple High School. By his own admission his school work had been suffering due to his deepening absorption with the band. Nevertheless, the previous year, he had gained enough qualifications to apply to enter Dublin's University College. Bono had commenced study there, but not for long. His place had subsequently been withdrawn when it was discovered that he had not passed his leaving Gaelic exam at Mount Temple.

The search for a direction in life would often weigh heavy on Bono; it formed the cornerstone of his songwriting and led him to explore many different experimental avenues. He was often confused and unconvinced by conventional religious teachings, and frequently intrigued by different faiths. In search of some answers, he began to attend meetings of a charismatic Dublin-based Christian group called Shalom.

In terms of religious background, U2 included two Protestants – Adam Clayton and the Edge. Bono had been raised as a Protestant and only Larry Mullen was a Roman Catholic. Now in his sincere commitment to the Shalom group Bono was joined by Larry Mullen and Edge; Adam Clayton, meanwhile, preferred to keep his distance. The three young men attended twice-weekly prayer meetings with the Shalom group, drawing – at least initially – sustenance from the experience.

No amount of religious fervour, however, could distract Bono from forging a career in music. On one level, he now saw it as his way out of the life that seemed to have been mapped out for him. The prospect of spending stultifying years in mundane employment, relieved only by weekend drinking sessions in a nearby local, appalled him.

But it was not the lurid hedonism synonymous with rock stardom that attracted Bono. He had a grander plan. He envisaged the role providing him with a vehicle for self-expression and a platform upon which to try to make a difference. These were lofty ambitions for an eighteen-year-old, doubtless frustrated by the slowness of the band's progress.

Meanwhile, U2 pressed on with securing local gigs. As summer arrived, they managed to staple themselves on to the bottom of the bill at McGonagle's, one of the capital city's leading clubs. This in turn led to a regular Thursday night spot at this venue.

On occasions, gigs could be a real baptism of fire. When U2 supported the Stranglers later in the year at the Top Hat Ballroom, they were spat at and had a range of missiles aimed at them on stage. But they kept their nerve.

They also showed a glimpse of things to come when they lent their support to a movement in Ireland that was protesting against the country's anti-contraception laws. The event, held in early 1978, was low-key, and the protest posters stuck on the wall behind the stage were home-made. They demanded 'Free Legal and Safe Contraception' in big, black hand-written letters on large sheets of white paper.

Months later, U2 showed up to perform at another local pub for a small action group that was protesting against sexism. But this gig was poorly supported, with only a few dozen attending.

Regardless of the audience size, Bono's performing style was memorable. His enthusiasm often got the better of him as he hurtled about in his as yet uncoordinated way, sometimes ruining the timing for the others. But he could also, on other occasions, be astonishingly riveting.

Visually he was untamed. His clump of dark, collar-length hair flopped across his brow and would end up in sweaty curls plastered to his face. Favouring roll-neck sweaters with the sleeves pushed up to the elbows and black shiny figure-hugging trousers, he cut a short stocky figure who practically lived in Cuban-heeled boots.

Away from performing, Bono enjoyed hanging out with Clayton, Mullen and Edge. Their ex-band mate, Dick Evans, had not dropped out of their circle either. Indeed, his room at Trinity College often served as a communal drop-in centre and meeting place.

Although several months had passed since the Limerick talent contest and their visit to Keystone Studios, CBS's Jackie Hayden had not forgotten about U2. In September 1978 he arranged for another demo session for the band, this time at Windmill Lane Studios in Dublin, with producer Chas de Whalley in charge.

Proof of the band's increased cohesion came when these sessions led to U2 landing a three-year recording contract with CBS Ireland. This welcome development, though, made no immediate difference to the band's life. U2 had not suddenly landed on their feet. A long road still stretched ahead and by now it was obvious that it was not going to be easy.

Although they secured some gigs playing support to the Stranglers and the Greedy Bastards, it was tough getting work. Rock music was not well served in the Republic of Ireland. There was an almost complete dearth of music media and concert amenities. A pirate radio station had been on the air for about a year. But there was still no national pop radio channel.

In the late seventies, polished, experienced, clean-cut show-bands who performed anodyne cover versions of popular standards had the monopoly on the local music scene. In truth, despite the recent emergence of the Boomtown Rats, a rock band was still something of an oddity in Dublin in those days.

Undaunted, U2 worked hard at honing their individual skills, while also crafting a group identity. All four agreed that rock music's selfish artifice held no attraction, even if – by standing clear of the traditional mire of indulgent excess – they risked costing the band an aura of mystique. Instead, they wanted U2's music to communicate a challenging social message and to do so with the kind of energy and power that would pack an unforgettable emotional punch.

A second demo recording session at Windmill Lane Studios in December produced better results. But their signing this year to CBS Ireland disappointingly remained unmatched by interest from CBS UK. But one thing was certain. Driven by a resilient belief in himself and in the band, with one foot firmly poised on the first rung of the ladder, Bono was going to be a hard man to keep down.

CHAPTER 3

Beginner

IN ADDITION TO EXPERIENCING some crushing moments during their earliest gigs, U2 made life even tougher for themselves by playing unfamiliar original material to audiences who were already ready to jeer and be hostile. Bono understood the jealousy that motivated these attacks. But he would not have been sorry to see the back of such bile by spring 1979, by which time, on the whole, their performances were beginning to produce a very different reaction.

At the turn of the previous year, the band had spent time assessing their strengths and acknowledging their weaknesses. This was not so much in an effort to accept their limitations as to find a realistic common reference point upon which they could then build. And it became a self-perpetuating cycle, as the Edge once explained: 'Our styles started developing *around* each other; a continual parallel development involving the songs, the musicianship and the styles.'

The reward was a uniquely identifiable sound and a tighter set. The band's burgeoning grass-roots support sprang up around the local youth centres and clubs, and developed into a cult following – courtesy of a small series of memorable gigs in a draughty, dank and derelict indoor car park near Dublin's St Stephen's Green.

Called the Dandelion, it was the city's hippest new focal point for Saturday afternoon sessions; the entrance fee was a mere 50 pence. The set-up was spartan, with a low, dilapidated wooden stage. And U2's less than state-of-the-art equipment was prone to break down, leaving Bono to hastily improvise. But it was one of the few places where U2 could perform for the benefit of the under-eighteens who were keen to see the band play, but who were not yet old enough to catch their pub and club gigs.

The concrete car park's austere surroundings might have seemed a barren setting. But, marked by an obvious precocity, the transparent honesty of U2's performances would soon establish their originality.

Unusually, too, with certain songs Bono conveyed little 'stories'. It was here, for instance, that he began what became a regular routine during the number 'Boy/Girl', producing an unlit cigarette and acting out the business of enjoying an illicit smoke. The intention was to illustrate, through this traditional teenage sneaky rebellion, the beginnings of the transition between boyhood and manhood.

It was in these unsalubrious surroundings, too, that Bono began to grow in stature. He still made uncompromising direct eye contact with people. And whenever he stepped up on stage, he first assumed a cloak of impressive importance. It was certainly a disproportionate importance at this point but still convincing.

At the core of his performance lay a relentless desire to closely interact with his audience. He worked hard at forging these ties but his excruciating sincerity – the antithesis of the currently popular cynicism – sometimes took U2 far out on a limb, almost to the point of embarrassment. And the emotionally charged atmosphere created at their gigs could have erratic results.

Uninhibited emotion has formed an integral part of Bono's stagecraft all his life and even in these early days he refused to hold back. Vocally, he could be, by turns, husky, melodic and plaintive. His hunger for attention was exaggerated and intense. By nakedly investing so much in his delivery, he placed his every mood swing on show, leaving the crowd to elect whether or not they wanted to share in that mood.

His blue-grey eyes (not yet hidden behind the dark glasses that he later adopted), his sensitive features, and his thick dark hair now swept down on to his collar together afforded him pin-up good looks that sat oddly against his often grave and idealistic attitude. All in all, Bono was no ordinary nineteen-year-old, as his songwriting clearly revealed.

At the start of the era that inspired Bono so much, Mick Jagger, along with Keith Richard, had been famously locked in a room for endless hours by Rolling Stones manager Andrew Loog Oldham in order to force them to focus on penning the band's first original compositions. Similarly, years later, Freddie Mercury started his songwriting career by joining in lively, sometimes protracted, brain-storming sessions with fellow Queen members.

But to Bono, then and now, inspiration for songs is a constantly fluid thing. This led him to adopt the nerve-racking habit of relying on his subconscious to hoard and formulate ideas, literally leaving it to the last minute to commit any lyrics to paper. This was a risky approach, especially when under pressure. Yet Bono produced remarkably thought-provoking material in this way.

It undoubtedly helped that Bono started out with an instinctive appreciation of language, and an innate grasp of its subtle nuances. His intention lyrically was to promote independence and freedom of thought, and to reject glossy, stereotyped media imagery. He also wanted to explore serious questions of spirituality – a subject avoided by most rock lyricists but one that Bono believed teenagers did think about, and one that should therefore be addressed. When all these elements were combined with his disconcerting ability to see beneath life's surface, his songs were bound to touch a nerve.

The first indication that Bono was interested in deeper issues than the standard hormonal yearnings familiar to teenagers, came with the song 'Out of Control'. It dealt with an eighteen-year-old's sudden realization that the two biggest events in a person's life – their birth and death – were out of their hands. By extension, it queried the very existence of free will. Bono had written this song on his own eighteenth birthday. It was an unusually sober reflection for a teenager and the song's unsettling anger, laced with a threatening doubt, was a precursor of things to come.

As early summer 1979 beckoned, the different sides of Bono's life were still jostling for space. Likewise, the maturing young men in U2 began to adopt their own individual lifestyles. Adam Clayton pursued the more expected route and enjoyed a lively social life amid the local pubs. Meanwhile, his bandmates were rarely to be found out on the town.

Far from behaving in the outrageous style of any self-respecting riotous rock band, Bono, Larry Mullen and the Edge continued to keep faith with the teachings of the Shalom group, part of whose ethos was to completely relinquish all vanity and ego. Edge was not a fanatical devotee. Neither really were Bono or Mullen. But the latter two were definitely more intensely involved than the guitarist chose to be.

Being in a rock band and at the same time attending private religious prayer and confession sessions laid them right open to the risk of ridicule. The whisper was already that U2 were born-again Christians. To Bono some subjects, however, are too important to go public on. He was not, and never would be, willing to discuss in any detail this particularly private part of his life.

In any event, Bono always preferred the focus to remain on the music. CBS Ireland had signed them months before, but to date they had nothing much to show for it. That contract covered the home territory but U2's vision was never limited to Ireland. They were always on the look-out for avenues through which they could showcase their talent further afield.

Back in February, they had had high hopes when they'd landed a spot at an all-night music event called 'Dark Space', staged at the Project Arts Centre. Attended by a journalist from Britain's *New Musical Express*, as well as the influential disc jockey John Peel (renowned for giving unknown bands a leg up), they thought it might have brought a breakthrough. But although U2 had played well on the night, it was not enough to attract Peel's patronage. And, while *NME* featured the 'Dark Space' event in it's next issue, U2 were not among the bands highlighted.

Nevertheless, positive thinking prevented despondency from setting in. Their manager Paul McGuinness went on the trail, knocking on London record company doors, clutching U2's first official demo tape (produced by Barry Devlin at the end of 1978). Meanwhile, Bono and the others concentrated on building their name and gathering experience. They would hold a post-mortem after each gig, dissecting their latest performance. On these occasions, all four could be unsparingly critical of themselves and of each other.

With Bono's need to be hands-on about everything, it was perhaps inevitable that, to supplement Paul McGuinness's efforts, he would want to throw himself into the task of trying to penetrate the London music scene. In April he managed to wangle his way to the UK capital.

Ostensibly, Bono was in London on behalf of *Hot Press* to review gigs by Thin Lizzy and Iggy Pop for the magazine. Once there, though, he also took the opportunity, in his spare time, to go round the music press offices, introducing himself and U2 to journalists, hoping to leave behind a favourable impression and to make a few useful contacts.

On his return to Dublin, Bono soon became completely absorbed in rehearsing and performing. Tangible proof that this hard work was paying dividends came when *Hot Press* declared in August, weeks before the band's first record release, 'No matter what band you play with south of the border, U2 can piddle all over you, lucrative publishing deals or not.'

Weeks later, in advance of that imminent record release, U2 had their first publicity photo shoot with freelance photographer Hugo McGuinness. Here too all four had creative ideas to offer. One of the more innovative to emerge was Bono's suggestion that if he dressed in white, while the other three wore black, then the singer would be clearly identifiable without having to be particularly prominent in every shot.

At long last, one year on from their signing with CBS Ireland, in September 1979, U2 made their recording debut with the release of the EP 'U2:3'. The A-side was 'Out of Control', backed by 'Stories for Boys' and 'Boy-Girl'.

Because of U2's steadily growing Irish support, and the band's existing profile in their own country, they had high expectations for the EP's performance. And there had been another fortuitous development.

RTE 2, a new Irish pop radio station, had lately been launched and, as a result of discussions with Paul McGuinness, the radio producer had agreed to run a poll inviting listeners to choose which of the three songs, intended for the EP, ought to be the lead track. 'Out of Control' had won the vote and in the process both the punters and the radio station personnel were left with the feeling that they had a vested interest in following the record's performance.

Cynics would say that this was a shrewd move on Paul McGuinness's part. But with U2 it is actually true that their intention from the outset was to encourage all-party involvement, thereby putting a human face on the business side of the music.

In addition to the conventional 7-inch vinyl edition of the EP, a 12-inch limited edition of 1,000 numbered copies was also released. Today, they are collector's items.

Not everyone was happy, however, to see U2 start to establish themselves. The band had built up a popular hometown following. But there was also a small group of people who resented them. A local gang spoiling for a fight had, throughout the summer, been targeting certain bands at their gigs, U2 among them.

At one gig, while U2 performed a support slot, Adam Clayton had suddenly had beer deliberately sloshed all over him just as a couple of dozen worked-up young men were lining up to rush on to the stage. The venue bouncers turfed the troublemakers out before they could further disrupt the gig, but not before Bono had armed himself with one of his heavy Cuban-heeled boots. On another occasion U2 had beer glasses tossed at them as they sat in a bar, minding their own business.

With his compact frame and his sturdy legs and arms, Bono is easily capable of wrestling a would-be attacker to the ground if need be. He had managed to exercise admirable patience in the past. But, furious at having to endure such behaviour once too often, Bono finally decided that enough was enough. Having recognized one particular gang member, he went looking for him to sort things out once and for all. Apparently, when he had tracked him down the hoodlum suddenly became squeamish at the prospect of squaring up to the clearly irate singer and fled.

Fortunately such distractions were rare and Bono could concentrate on the important things in life, such as U2's first record. Released only in Ireland it was no surprise when 'U2:3' topped the national singles chart. Like the others, however, Bono continued to hanker after chart success in Britain.

That task looked to be an uphill struggle on their first UK incursion, financed by some of the band's family members and friends. During this visit they played an almost nightly string of dates in various London clubs and ballrooms over the first fortnight in December 1979, but failed to arouse even a faint ripple of interest. At one gig in Islington the band were barely outnumbered two to one by the audience. And the music press, despite recent attempts to woo them, totally ignored U2.

Spirits swiftly lifted, though, in the new year, for in January U2 walked off with the top prize in five separate categories at the annual *Hot Press* readers poll awards. Beating such established bands as

Thin Lizzy and the Boomtown Rats, their success was quickly consolidated when they performed live on TV's *The Late Show* and played to sell-out audiences during a short Irish tour. Then they notched up a second chart-topper on 26 February 1980 with the single 'Another Day'/'Twilight'. Once again their record label covered only the Irish market, but momentum was gathering.

Two or three major British record labels were by now starting to take notice of U2. For a while, EMI was thought to be the most serious. But, by the end of February, their interest had evaporated. This let-down severely dented the band's confidence, especially as they were suffering real financial hardship at the time.

It was a low point, but, operating on the premise that an aura of success breeds success, they concluded that projecting a facade of strength and brimming confidence was the best antidote to their predicament. Consequently, they organized a series of gigs around Ireland, culminating with a headline appearance at Dublin's national stadium. Their recent sweep at the *Hot Press* awards had helped to justify securing such a slot. And the strategy worked. It was at this prestigious venue that the band received an important backstage visitor.

He was Bill Stewart, head of A&R for the UK record label Island Records. A couple of Stewart's colleagues, including his deputy Annie Roseberry, had reported favourably on an earlier recent U2 performance. Then, while attending the national stadium gig he recognized the band's potential for himself. Backstage, in their dressing room, Bill Stewart offered U2 a deal in principle that night, with the terms to be negotiated. And U2 *wanted* to negotiate.

Even though they were financially up against the wall, and aware that they were in no position to make demands on the only record company that was talking to them, Bono and the others fought for, and won, a greater degree of creative control to be sewn into the deal.

Island Records' ethos of encouraging articulate, independently minded artistes meant that it was a marriage of minds. On 23 March 1980, in London, both sides were happy to officially commit to a four-year deal, with the customary option to extend that period. The documents were signed at the Lyceum where U2 were performing. Weirdly, the actual signing took place in the privacy of the ladies toilets.

This major international recording contract covered all territories except the Irish market. (Here, CBS Ireland continued to control the rights to U2's music for a few years.) It opened the door to a shining future, but Bono's first emotion was more one of short-term relief. He was grateful, he said, to have the money to be able to get back home to Ireland.

Every year, tens of thousands of artistes seek a record deal. Out of these, probably less than a couple of hundred will succeed. Partly what had marked U2 out had been their undiluted passion and their joint commitment. Years later, Island Records' founder Chris Blackwell confirmed, 'They're very fervent about their music. They're a real group. They move and think as one unit.' Significantly, he also stressed how impressed he had been with each of the four individuals on a personal level.

Once back in Dublin, the band spent the Easter break at Windmill Lane Studios recording their debut Island Records single '11 O'Clock Tick Tock'/'Touch'. Released in Britain on 23 May 1980, the A-side was a high-voltage number dealing with the prospect of the world facing its eleventh hour.

The band backed the single with a tour which began at the Hope and Anchor pub in London and visited various cities around England before returning to the capital, where it ended on 8 June at the Half Moon Club in Herne Hill. Despite their efforts, the single failed to make the UK charts.

But at the crucial point of live contact between artiste and audience, U2 were unmistakably thriving, and their fan base was consequently swelling. Although Bono still tended to be slightly awkward on stage, he was growing more familiar with his role as the band's primary lightning rod.

He was also emerging as the natural magnet for journalists. Always loquacious, he talked intensely to anyone who was willing to listen about the need for a new direction in music, for a departure from the tired old themes. His outspokenness swiftly became apparent.

He did not restrict his pronouncements to musical issues either. For example, he baldly articulated the hypocrisy of governments which advocated a healthy lifestyle, while at the same time making a mint from tobacco and alcohol tax revenue. Bono had realized that he had a platform for his views and he was more than willing to use it.

Barely past his twentieth birthday, he openly derided the reckless 'let's get wasted' lifestyle notoriously adopted by young rock stars. He admitted to enjoying an occasional drink, but clearly found the practice of pondering life's complexities far more intoxicating than alcohol. Even so, he was always aware of the risk of appearing puritanical. To the curious press, just getting to know him, Bono represented an intriguing challenge.

Here was a young songwriter willing to tackle impenetrable subjects – such as faith and death – that many older lyricists shied away from. They also found his insatiable inquisitiveness and his brutal candour refreshing. And he was articulate and intelligent. These early encounters formed the basis of what would become a positive relationship with the media.

With the pace of life hotting up, much of the next six months would be spent either on the road or in the recording studio. In July, U2 played three gigs in London, followed by two Dublin appearances. In the latter they joined bands the Squeeze and the Police in the city's Dalymount Festival, before finding themselves closeted once again in Windmill Lane Studios.

August saw the release of 'A Day Without Me'/'Things To Make and Do', with the lead track continuing the band's preoccupation with spirituality and morality (the lyrics dealt graphically with the emotional aftermath of a suicide). It also marked the beginning of work on U2's debut album. Entering the studio with the general framework already mapped out, Bono composed – as usual – on the mike.

It was an intense and productive time, within a very short timescale – determined by the start of the next tour. It would be a bigger onslaught this time, once again stretching the length and breadth of England. Playing such diverse venues as Demelza's in Penzance and London's famous Marquee, the tour commenced in early September in Coventry. It ended on 19 October when U2 played support to the 1970s hit glam band Slade at London's Lyceum Ballroom, before paying a brief visit to Europe for the remainder of the month.

It was a month in which they had already notched up yet another single 'I Will Follow', backed by a live version of 'Boy-Girl', which was released in Britain and, for the first time, also in America. October 1980 also saw the release of U2's debut album *Boy*.

The short-haired, bare-chested young boy, standing with both hands placed trustingly behind his head, who was pictured on the UK album cover, was Peter Rowan, the younger brother of Bono's friend Guggi. The band had sought to encapsulate *Boy*'s concept of innocence, and unblemished purity indeed shone from his improbably large, almond-shaped clear eyes. It was an arresting photograph, turned into a striking image.

Adam Clayton would later stress how vital it had been to them all for the cover to strike an instantly emotive note. 'We weren't mindless punks just into rebellion,' he said. Neither had they wanted to be marketed as a pop band. It had been Bono's idea to feature a photograph of the eight-year-old child on the sleeve instead of themselves. And this had partly served to avoid revealing just how young the band members were.

The unique cover (which twenty years later would make it into a

Q magazine poll of the Hundred Best Record Covers of All Time) excited a degree of positive comment. In America, however, the record company decided to change it for another sleeve, as they were slightly concerned that unwelcome overtones could be wrongly attributed to it.

Bono remarked at the time that the sight of the watchful child on the cover invariably prompted him to wonder what the boy's future would be – just as he wondered about U2's long-term prospects at this, the outset of their recording career.

By contrast, he had no doubts about what the band wanted the album's contents to convey. Years later, Larry Mullen spoke of U2 having emerged out of the punk rock era. But, while the band agreed with the principle of individualism, they flatly rejected the violence that was inextricably associated with punk. Instead, they strove to create an aura of hope.

In the then climate of mass unemployment and fast-spreading disillusionment in British society, Bono declared that, far from letting negativity take hold, U2's music was meant to be about getting up and doing something about it.

Produced by Steve Lillywhite, the album's refreshing original-ity would broadly find favour with the critics. But it was not so well received commercially. *Boy* took almost a year to reach number fifty-two in the British charts. It would also stall at sixty-three in America where *Rolling Stone* later commented, 'The songs – mostly chronicles of psychic growing pains – are a diffuse and uneven lot'. However, the magazine still credited U2 as being 'potentially exceptional'.

Following hard on the heels of another four-week trek around Britain, during which they had supported the group Talking Heads at the Hammersmith Palais and the Odeon in London, in late November 1980 U2 played their first ever American gigs – a selec-tion of club dates on the eastern seaboard.

They opened in Boston, and if they had been apprehensive about what kind of reception to expect, all their fears were allayed. From practically the first note ringing out, the packed club was heaving with sweaty, excited people, scaring up a storm that left the band as exhilarated as its frenzied audience. The crowd's appetite for U2 was voracious. They demanded at least three encores. A breathless, pumping Bono eventually turned to Edge and declared that, if this was a true taste of America, then bring it on.

Nevertheless, as 1980 drew to a close, the fact of the matter was that not one of U2's three Island Records' singles had charted in Britain and their debut album could hardly be classed as a commercial world-beater. Yet none of this dimmed Bono's desire for the band to become, creatively, the best rock act in the world *and*, crucially, to achieve this without sacrificing an ounce of artistic integrity. There were already those in the music business who were watching closely, interested to see whether or not such a goal was attainable.

CHAPTER 4

Acolyte

IN DECEMBER 1980 John Lennon was murdered outside his home in New York City by a young man who, having asked the ex-Beatle hours earlier for his autograph, had then chillingly lain in wait with a loaded gun for the star's return. This tragedy had forced many in a suddenly jittery rock world to re-evaluate not only their personal security arrangements but, in a broader sense, the meaning of fame.

The shooting that so shocked the world undoubtedly affected Bono, especially at a time when he was already questioning whether the pursuit of fame was a spiritually worthwhile ambition. Superstar status was, as yet, a far distant aspiration. But in February 1981 Bono was boldly predicting to journalists that, because of their special chemistry, U2 were destined to join the ranks of rock royalty. Yet the moment his feet were set on a path towards achieving this, his doubts began.

The main problem was how to reconcile his Christian beliefs, and his faithful following of the Shalom group's teachings, with a desire to reach a privileged position. As a fêted rock idol, he would inevitably be tempted to live a life of reckless dissipation. It was a conflict of conscience that would take Bono some time to resolve.

In the meantime, as spring 1981 approached, U2 were firmly back in harness. Having spent most of the opening months of the year on the road in Britain and around Europe, in March they embarked on a major tour of North America and Canada. Kicking off in Washington DC, they played fifty-six dates in twenty-seven states over a three-month period.

Their spiritual doubts appeared to be in abeyance for the moment, with Bono brashly announcing that he was heading to America to, 'give it what I consider it wants and needs'.

Although the tour was well funded and well organized, they had set themselves a tough itinerary. The record company worked hard to win U2 the vital oxygen of radio airplay. As the band criss-crossed the country, Island Records' efforts to stir up sufficient pre-publicity to pave the way for their arrival in each town had varying degrees of success.

For the four in the spotlight it was challenging. Raw chemistry nightly energized band and crowd alike in an exhilarating, shared experience that was also extremely draining. But, through it, the whole unit grew stronger, more mature and more confident.

They were on solid ground. Americans traditionally like their rock music to be patently heterosexual, so they responded positively to U2's hard sound. Equally, US audiences were not particularly fazed by any Christian elements. And, despite the distinct darkness of some songs, U2 were largely an optimistic band which also found favour.

Every rock audience has its own personality and Bono was becoming adept at sensing the mood each night. He had the knack of stoking the interest of their existing fans, while also beguiling and persuading the curious newcomers who were being drawn in increasing numbers to the fold. He was not coy about his or the band's enthusiasm for the United States. And the naturally demonstrative Americans responded positively to a singer who was willing to wear his heart so openly on his sleeve.

It was U2's longest sustained foreign stint on the road yet and life was a constant whirl. In their free time they were keen to meet the music business fraternity and they spent hours pressing the flesh, getting themselves known. They wanted to spread the word that not only could they do their stuff on stage, but that they were also a positive thinking band with whom people could work well.

In city after city, their backstage dressing room would fill up with potential contacts, record company personnel and some enterprising fans who had managed to give security the slip. Networking was an exhausting business. With little or no time to downshift from the emotional high produced by performing, a still wired Bono normally plunged heartily into the hand-shaking, fast-talking melée. But occasionally he had to take himself off the merry-go-round, and slip away, for some time alone.

Strain can take many different forms. And by the time the tour was nearly two-thirds in, Bono's voice began to act up, with his delivery getting progressively huskier. Other tensions also crept in. While the cliché that travel broadens the mind remained true, in this case, travelling crammed sardine-fashion into a van had a decidedly claustrophobic effect on the four friends. To alleviate the stress, they took a short break which they spent in the Bahamas. Then it was back to work.

Overall, the trip could be accounted a success. They had attracted reasonable to good-sized crowds. They had been discovered by some of the musically minded Irish expatriates in America. And, in places, they had earned themselves three or more encores at the end of their fifty-minute sets.

Bono passed the milestone of his twenty-first birthday while he was in America's Deep South and the tour ended three weeks later in Asbury Park, New Jersey, at the end of May. Gigging was not quite over yet though for, within days of returning home in June, they proceeded to honour three British concert dates in Salford, Aylesbury and London.

At this point Bono would have been entitled to feel a degree of contentment, particularly when 'Fire'/'J. Swallo', which had been recorded at Compass Point Studios in Nassau during their Bahamas sojourn, entered the UK singles charts on 8 August at number thirty-nine. It then peaked three weeks later at four places higher, at last giving U2 their British Top 40 chart debut.

But, as the band swapped the rigours of touring for the confines of the studio to concentrate on making their second album, they began a time of deep soul-searching and confusion.

Bono later admitted that, for a good couple of years or so from this point, for himself, Edge and Larry Mullen, spirituality would be the dominant force in life. He described himself as becoming completely wrapped up in it, and it gave rise to some friction. Because this commitment to spirituality and to the Shalom group was not shared by Adam Clayton, as a band they had to battle against the very real risk of the bass player becoming isolated musically, as well as in other ways.

The same solid core of three who were unified religiously, were also each emotionally settled in steady relationships. Meanwhile, Clayton was still happy to be footloose. Consequently, he continued to lead a very different lifestyle.

Nothing felt straightforward to Bono. Looking back, he has described this period as a 'crisis of identity'. Were they Christians in a rock band, or were they a Christian rock band? And, on top of that, the continuing struggle to square the circle over the merits of being in a rock band at all, raged on.

Eventually they came to the point where they did not know if they wanted to make another record. The music world seemed so ruthless and shallow. By contrast, the people with whom Bono, Larry Mullen and Edge were involved spiritually appeared to be far more worthy, with aims that were so much more worthwhile.

These destabilizing feelings went on for some time and they went very deep – Bono later revealed that, between the release of their second album and writing their third album, the band performed each gig on the unspoken four-way mutual assumption that it might be their last ever performance. Such uncertainty must have been extremely unnerving.

Adam Clayton later cited this same period as the time when U2 could have contemplated breaking up. Edge has confessed that he inwardly queried whether or not he truly wanted to be part of the rock scene. He declared, 'We had to figure out where we were going.'

And Bono became so torn between his religious commitment and being in a band that he seriously considered quitting U2. His plight was not helped by the contradictory feelings he experienced. He wanted the interaction and the contact with fans, but the usual outward affirmation of rising popularity normally craved by young rock stars – being mobbed by overheated girls in a frenzy, or suffocated by frantic autograph hunters – often dismayed Bono. In the same way, he had been disturbed by the whole gladiatorial aura of rock performances and the corresponding audience adulation.

It was not a customary dilemma for a rock star, and Bono took time to come to his decision. But in the end he and the band decided that a compromise was possible. The three practising Christians would pursue musical success, but in doing so they would studiously shun its traditional pitfalls – the over-indulgence in drink and wild womanizing. Instead, they would use any fame they attained as an active power for good.

Bono's social conscience had already led him to join a party of helpers who offered practical assistance to the overstretched staff of a Dublin drop-in centre for down-and-outs. Not yet in a position to make a substantial financial contribution to worthwhile causes, he still wanted to help.

There was nothing cosmetic or superficial about Bono's determination to confront the underbelly of life. And this impulse would find its way into the already religious direction of the material that would form U2's next album.

Called *October* and recorded at Windmill Lane Studios, the album's anthem-like tracks contained innumerable references to Jesus Christ. Its theme was the journey of life – from undergoing trials and tribulations to achieving subsequent spiritual recovery. Released in October 1981, it performed appreciably better than its predecessor, *Boy*, reaching number eleven in Britain. Inevitably, though, *October* branded U2 with a religious stigma.

Bono was very aware that the press would try to make an issue of the unusual fact that three members of U2 were committed Christians. And he wanted to prevent that particular balloon taking off. On the other hand, he was prepared to risk turning the focus on to the issue by openly commenting on the, by and large, non-acceptance of religion as a valid feature in popular music. He pointed out succinctly that, in terms of rock lyric writing, perverted sado-masochism was not off-limits, but that, curiously, spirituality was.

Disappointingly, the album failed to spawn the hit single that was now anticipated by many music industry insiders. 'Gloria'/'I Will Follow (live)', released in mid-October, slipped back from the band's earlier single's success and stalled at number fifty-five. And the fervour of *October* did not catch fire in America where the album missed getting into the Top 100. However, none of this dampened Bono's expectation of being able to build upon the previous positive inroads made in the US where, by now, U2 were touring once again.

A handful of gigs back in August, kicked off by an appearance at Slane Castle, near Dublin, and followed by an eighteen-date British tour launched on 1 October, had tuned U2 up nicely for this fresh round of American gigs. This time their tour stretched from Albany in New York State on 13 November, to Hartford, Connecticut, on 12 December.

They introduced into their set the new material from *October*. But, although a committed Christian, Bono was not on a crusade to convert the masses. And neither had his personal beliefs in any way subdued his effervescent sense of humour. Out-takes of an appearance that U2 recorded during this tour, for the popular satellite music channel MTV, show Bono in playful mood, exercising his quick wit and boyish charm before a floor producer who seemed not entirely appreciative of the singer's irrepressible spirit.

Indeed, inexhaustible stamina was badly needed. Having already spent most of the year on the road, the band left America in time to perform two more gigs before Christmas at London's Lyceum. These were followed, early in 1982, by three Irish gigs, in Galway, Cork, and the Royal Dublin Society Hall.

January's Dublin appearance represented the pinnacle of what had been a hugely successful return to their homeland for U2. Fresh from acquiring yet more honours at the annual *Hot Press* awards, they played to a five thousand capacity crowd that fully reciprocated their explosive enthusiasm. The emotional interaction with the audience that night left Bono breathless.

Equally, his apprehension at the band's evolving status still preoccupied him. Away from the stage, if ambushed by fans, Bono liked to *talk* to them. When they started to grab at him, wanting to tear bits off his clothes, it gave him serious pause for thought.

Change was inevitable with their growing fame, and U2's fan base had also altered with *October*'s release. The band's unwavering desire to plough its own furrow, and to push their music on in new directions, was bound to bring casualties. The new album, while gaining U2 new fans, drawn by its overtly religious content, also cost the band fans, who were turned off by those same tones.

Likewise, a degree of territoriality among original U2 grass-roots supporters led some of them to dislike the band's rising popularity, preferring the preservation of cult status over the prospect of mass appreciation. But Bono had little patience with, what he bluntly termed, 'elitist followers'. U2 planned to keep changing and evolving musically, no matter what anyone thought.

The paucity of major singles success in Britain thus far did not particularly bother the band, nor their record company. It already seemed obvious that their strength lay in albums and in live concert appearances. The fact was that U2 never intended to become a singles band. That said, it was mainly the generous airplay of all their singles on MTV that was helping to build the band a cult Stateside following. This became obvious when they arrived in America in February 1982 for their fourth tour of the country in fourteen months. One of the highlights of this tour would be a gig on 17 March at the Ritz, a popular New York City rock venue.

This had not originally been the band's plan for St Patrick's Day. The celebration of Ireland's patron saint is an occasion marked in America by massive street parades which assume a carnival atmosphere. There are marching bands, bright costumes and a stream of gigantic, imaginative and colourful floats.

New York's famous St Patrick's Day parade traditionally passes along the city's chic Fifth Avenue and attracts enormous public and media attention. With U2 touring the United States, pushing their new album, Paul McGuinness had thought it would be a great promotional idea to secure the band a float on which to perform live through the streets. Bono and the others were looking forward to it.

But, as the event drew near, it was then discovered that the parade's honorary marshal for this year looked likely to be named as Bobby Sands (a member of the Provisional IRA, who had died the year before while on a hunger strike, as part of a campaign for the reinstatement of political prisoner status).

Some Irish expatriates in the US may have considered Bobby Sands to be a martyr. But U2, who already despaired of the perpetual fighting between Protestants and Catholics in Northern Ireland, could not support IRA tactics. The prospect that Bobby Sands could be confirmed as the honorary marshal for this event – thereby politicizing it – was enough for them to withdraw from taking part in the parade. It was unfortunate, but unavoidable. A fortnight later, U2 returned to Dublin just in time for the UK release on 3 April of 'A Celebration'/'Trash', which fizzled out at number forty-seven.

The adrenalin rush of constant live performances, coupled with the stimulation of ever-shifting landscapes, can be intoxicating. But Bono was aware that the band needed to steady up and retrench once again. For this they chose their long-term professional base, Windmill Lane Studios. Here, with the exception of a few sporadic one-off gigs, they spent the entire summer recording new material.

This period was their longest spell in Dublin for quite a while. But the itinerant life Bono had been leading, his absorption in music, had not prevented him from nurturing his relationship with his long-term girlfriend Alison Stewart. Though Bono would later acknowledge the difficulty of maintaining a sound personal commitment when one half of the couple is regularly away from home, he admitted that the key to success largely lay in the strength of the woman to cope.

With Adam Clayton as his best man, Bono married Alison Stewart in a traditional service on 21 August 1982 at the Church of Ireland in Raheny, Dublin. Strong-minded and smart, Alison would from the start independently carve out her own path. This included involvement in various issues, some of which overlapped with those with which Bono was involved, but not all.

As the wife of a rising rock star she also made other clear-cut decisions. For instance, from the outset (with very few exceptions), she would always prefer to keep out of the limelight, keen to preserve her own space and privacy, as well as her individual identity. At the same time, though, she would be extremely supportive of Bono's career. To many around them they were a couple who were ideally suited.

Bono's professional commitments, however, meant that before long he rejoined the rest of the band in the studio. Here, having finally resolved their personal dilemmas about their chosen career, their new material was beginning to take shape.

Their individual and collective concentration on weightier matters than would normally preoccupy a band whose average age was around twenty-one, has been described by Bono as growing up in a 'distorted way'. Certainly, U2 and Bono now began to take a socio-political lyrical stance, joining the voices that were clamouring for peace in Northern Ireland and a brighter future for its people.

In this regard, Bono had forged an unusual alliance. It had begun earlier in the year when, returning from Europe, U2 had found themselves in the same Heathrow Airport departure lounge as Garret Fitzgerald, leader of the Fine Gael political party, then campaigning in the 1982 general election.

Bono had promptly buttonholed the senior Irish politician and held him in close conversation about Ireland's various problems as they had waited to board the aircraft – a conversation that carried on throughout the entire flight to Dublin.

Garret Fitzgerald recalls the incident thus:

Bono and his band were coming back from England. I was waiting to board the plane and he recognized me. He wanted to talk to me, so he came over and just sat down beside me. I asked him what he did and he told me and we got talking, at first about things generally. I found him very interesting. He was clearly a person with a good mind, a serious person who is interested in politics and in all kinds of issues.

By touchdown the two men had formed a contact strong enough for them to promise to keep in touch with each other in the coming months.

However, U2 are careful not to align themselves with any particular political party. Their association with Garret Fitzgerald was a personal endorsement of the man himself, not necessarily an endorsement of every aspect of Fine Gael's policies.

On his return to the studio, shortly after his marriage, Bono invited Garret Fitzgerald to Windmill Lane. This visit, very late in the election campaign, was duly witnessed by a posse of puzzled journalists and photographers.

The appeal of courting the youth vote through rock music stars was becoming more recognized. Garret Fitzgerald says, 'Bono spoke favourably about my party during the election and that was politically helpful.' For his part, Bono was keen to engage in dialogue with, prospectively, the man who would have the power to actively make a difference in the country.

By defeating his opponent Charles Haughey and his Fianna Fail party, Garret Fitzgerald became Ireland's Taoiseach soon afterwards. A year later Bono would be invited by the Prime Minister to take part in a Select Government Action Committee on Unemployment. Garret Fitzgerald explains, 'Having started the youth employment scheme we needed some people to help run it and because I already had this contact with Bono I asked him to do it.'

The singer assumed this new role with his customary zeal, only to – inevitably – run into the brick wall of convention. He wanted the select committee to personally consult with real people who were currently unemployed or struggling as single parents, to physically invite them to the table to learn from them first-hand about their problems. This idea met with concerted resistance from the rest of the committee: it was not the way things were normally done. Such a rigid approach, and the formal structure of the meetings, were too restricting for Bono and he reluctantly quit.

His main aim was now to express his acute consciousness of Ireland's troubles, both political and social, in his lyrics. Accordingly, in October 1982, at a gig in Belfast he introduced, for the first time, a song called 'Sunday Bloody Sunday'.

Over the years, Edge would be crucial to the creation of much of the band's music. He would also often come up with an inspirational title or an opening line upon which Bono would go to work to develop a song. 'Sunday Bloody Sunday' was originally an idea that came to the guitarist while Bono was away on his honeymoon.

At his seaside home, Edge had been writing music for a new number when it had struck him out of the blue that the lyrics for it ought to be about Northern Ireland. Edge later explained, 'I wrote down a few lines and Bono instantly improved on them when he came back.'

Bloody Sunday was the name given to the infamous incident that had occurred ten years earlier, on 30 January 1972, during a civil rights demonstration in the Bogside that had turned into a riot. British paratroopers on duty in Londonderry had shot dead thirteen people and wounded a further seventeen.

Working fast on the song, Bono and the Edge had taken this incendiary moment in Ireland's bloody history and thought to twin it in some way with the blood spilled by Jesus Christ at his crucifixion. It was what Bono came to call 'a highfalutin idea'. He also came to believe that the intended meaning of the song was ultimately missed by many people.

'Sunday Bloody Sunday' was a fierce pounding number, punctuated by military-style staccato drumming. Bono introduced it at that Belfast gig as being a song of 'hope and of disgust', and it became a powerful anthem and one of U2's most famous songs. Bono's passionate delivery of this song also marked the start of him being perceived as an issues man. This was a mantle that he accepted, though it would prove burdensome at times.

CHAPTER 5

Revolutionary

REAL **REVOLUTION RESIDED** in refusing to compromise conscience, Bono believed. Busily stoking his internal fire, he would become inflamed by the conflicts and injustices going on in the world around him. And he would express these concerns not only through the medium of his music but also in interviews, as his public profile inexorably grew.

The media always loves an assertive personality and Bono could pontificate with the best of them. Not shy of branding the music scene, as at spring 1983, as being 'full of shit', he also fired a broadside at U2's contemporaries, condemning in general terms the trend towards vacuous posers who projected style over substance.

In contrast to the sort of highly stylized image then favoured by pop acts, none of the members of U2 could be accused of being a fashion plate. Distinctly dressed down and at times in funereal black, Bono took to cramming on top of his long hair a series of stark wide-brimmed hats. For years, these hats would be his trademark.

The frontman announced that music needed to be woken up and given an injection of much-needed gravitas. And that gravitas was to be provided by U2. Confident before television cameras, with his talkative, machine-gun manner, Bono was fond of quoting John

Lennon's earlier description of rock music as having become 'wall-paper music' – pretty and well designed. Bono now decided that even punk rock had, to some extent, been contrived and he called for a return to the garage band tradition when people played real instruments, with a passion.

In reproving tones he specifically pointed to the bad habit which some pop stars had developed of showing their backs to the audience. U2, on the other hand, he proudly declared, was all about communication.

Evidence that they were getting their message across came with the 22 January release of the single, 'New Year's Day'/'Treasure' which rewarded the band with their first UK Top 10 hit when it peaked at number ten in early February. And this achievement was quickly eclipsed by the release the following month of their third album, entitled *War*, which pulled off the enviable feat of entering the British chart at number one. Bono and the others received the happy news whilst on a sell-out tour which had commenced in Scotland in late February 1983 and was winding its way around Britain.

In reviewing U2's previous work, *October*, rock critic Jon Pareles for *Rolling Stone* had caustically wished Bono 'a speedy recovery from adolescence' and had expressed the hope that, next time, the band would find a suitable outlet for all their angst.

War was much more than that. It would bring widespread acknowledgement as being U2's most fully realized and fulfilling album to date. It had a gutsier, far darker sound and it represented a significant advance both conceptually and technically.

The lyrics talked about the emotions inherent in conflict, the abuse of power and the damage done, and they challenged the mindless generational following of footsteps that perpetuated a never-ending cycle of hatred. The lyrics also exhorted listeners to have the courage to move out from behind the traditional barricades of suspicion. And they attempted to personalize the face of strife in the Middle East, the Falklands, and the Solidarity movement in Poland, as well as highlighting the arms race and the ever-present nuclear threat. They also focused on the sectarian violence in Northern Ireland.

The album cover was, once again, immensely striking. Peter Rowan had returned, this time obviously slightly older, in a full face close-up shot which showed an angry, piercing stare. The inspiration behind the choice of cover is said to have come from wartime images of Nazis rounding up Jewish children.

In certain countries – notably America where *War* reached number twelve – U2 began to be viewed as a political band. But Bono maintained that *War* was an emotional, rather than a political, work. Emotions certainly ran amok in Bono's delivery, leading one critic to describe his vocals as 'a stuttering rage'.

Perhaps inevitably, the album's lead track, 'Sunday Bloody Sunday', provoked the most vivid response. As a result, a slew of misconceptions had to be clarified. It was not a pro-Irish, pro-violence song. It was an anti-war statement.

Commentators also quickly questioned how someone from Eire could feel entitled to write about the murderous mayhem that blighted Northern Ireland. Bluntly, Bono stated that, while the explosions were not going off in Dublin, the devastating explosive devices were certainly made in Dublin. Moreover, the defiant, straight-talking 23-year-old declared that being an Irishman in itself gave him the right to speak out.

The whole issue of Northern Ireland and religiously motivated conflict was a thorny one. On occasions, though, even the quiet and normally reserved Larry Mullen felt driven to air his personal views. He would challenge head-on the hypocrisy of any of the warring factions which tried to claim some kind of moral high ground. As he pointed out, individual faction members would worship in church and then promptly go out and commit cold-blooded, premeditated murder.

U2 remained unequivocal that they did not take sides and they would rail against *all* killing and examples of bigotry or intolerance. Although raised in the Protestant faith, Bono did not consider the Protestant church's teachings to be infallible. It was important to him to feel that, if he chose to, he could go into a Catholic church; not that he considered Catholicism to be an ideal doctrine either. But his own parents' mixed marriage had given him proof that the two religions could live side-by-side in harmony.

During live performances of 'Sunday Bloody Sunday' Bono would reinforce the song's anti-violence stand by wrapping himself in a white flag as he sang. He also rejected point blank the notion that recording an album which examined such serious subject matter meant that U2 had somehow revealed a preoccupation with depressing negativity.

However, for Bono, there *was* a moment just after *War*'s release that was both negative and depressing, the memory of which would torment him for a long time afterwards.

It was tragically all too common to hear news reports during the Irish Troubles of anonymous gunmen materializing at someone's home, shooting dead the husband or father, brother or son in the house, and then vanishing into the night.

Soon after the emergence of the song 'Sunday Bloody Sunday', one day Bono became instantly uneasy at the sight of two men who had appeared on foot close to the door of the beach house which he and Ali shared. The two men were armed and wore military-style berets, but the singer's gut instinct was that they were not from the official authorities.

His next unbidden instinct was to get a large knife from a drawer in the kitchen. But, whoever the men were, the moment passed without incident. Left staring down at the glinting weapon grasped firmly in his hand, the grim evidence that, if necessary, he – a firm pacifist – had been prepared to protect his family by using violence, appalled Bono. Relating the story several years later, he revealed in a *Rolling Stone* magazine interview (8 October 1997) that

that one natural action had sickened him and that he had been left feeling a hypocrite.

Leaving aside *War*'s content, the album's style was a clear departure from that of its two predecessors. Bono admitted that they had consciously veered away from the expected U2 sound towards a stark, stripped-down format.

It had proved to be a wise decision. This, their strongest album yet, placed them in a nice bargaining position just as the time came to start renegotiating their recording deal with Island Records. The upshot was that U2 would acquire ownership of all of their songs – and in time this would make wealthy men of all four of them.

The increased attention that came with success, however, did not always elicit the expected reaction. It's the lot of any frontman to become the central focus of a band and Bono, through his penchant for making fearless pronouncements, gave every indication of being happy with that.

Yet, as *War*'s success turned a brighter spotlight on to him than ever before, Bono confessed to becoming, as he put it, 'fed up with being Bono'. He would prefer it, he revealed, if the other three band members were given more prominence.

There seemed to be sufficient prominence to go around. After chalking up a number eighteen UK hit with the single 'Two Hearts Beat As One'/'Endless Deep', released on 2 April, the band faced the prospect of embarking on a two-month tour of predominantly American arenas, ending in early June.

By the midway point in the US itinerary, U2 had made their American singles' chart debut with 'New Year's Day'. It rose no higher than number fifty-three, but this belied the great strides in popularity which U2 were making in the flesh there. Whether in New York State, North Carolina, Michigan or Philadelphia, they drew large audiences and great reviews.

In terms of experience, this tour was invaluable and their performances this time around ranked as some of their most memorable. One of these high points occurred at the end of May 1983, in the three-day US festival held at San Bernardino in California. Another took place days later, at Red Rocks Amphitheatre in Denver, Colorado.

This outdoor craggy natural setting would have been dramatic enough without the overcast weather spreading a canopy of threatening black clouds that brought torrential rain. This meant that the saturated stage had to be swept clear of water before the band could play. In the misty dark night, bathed only in the orange glow given off by massive flame torches on towers positioned around the stage, they had an ethereal appearance which added further resonance to the music.

That night U2 played a dynamic set that confirmed them as a top-notch live rock act and also showcased their individual style. Where Freddie Mercury preened and paraded, and Mick Jagger strutted about, poking his chest and chin out, Bono's style, mid-1980s was a gentler, jaunty, skip-hop gambol.

Tripping close to the lip of the stage, he darted among the sea of outstretched grasping hands. At one point he allowed himself to casually fall backwards off the stage and into the crowd's safe-keeping, confident that the same forest of upturned hands would willingly support his body weight. And at the end of a high-voltage rendition of 'Sunday Bloody Sunday' he fell to one knee, his forearms crossed on one tightly clad thigh and, slightly out of breath, gazed over the appreciatively roaring crowd.

Before the tour, Bono had boasted, 'There's no stage big enough for me,' meaning that no stage could match his desire to communicate with every person in the audience. It was no surprise, therefore, that oftentimes, as they gigged around America, Bono could end up anywhere in the auditorium.

The near nightly gigs in 2,000 to 12,000-seater venues had become highly energizing affairs. Seemingly inexhaustible, the band gave their all. And, through their own collective commitment, they fused the individuals beyond the footlights into one concentrated excitable mass.

Over the weeks, U2 had taken to displaying white flags on tall poles on stage. At a particular point in the show it became a ritual that Bono would pass one of these flags down into the crowd. The fans would pass it around among themselves before duly handing it back to Bono, in an expression of unity.

In Seattle one night Bono decided to take making contact to the logical extreme. He vanished from the stage, only to reappear in the midst of the heaving mass of bodies, microphone in hand and still singing. It was potentially a dangerous stunt but the fans closest to him hoisted him up to lie horizontal on his back. Like this, they then passed him over a succession of hands and heads safely back to the stage. Other times, Bono expressed his need for contact by pulling a girl at random up from the crowd to dance with her for a while. All these actions only intensified the fans' hysteria.

The white flags Bono brandished were supposed to symbolize sanity. But one night, in a few moments of madness, sanity went out of the window and the gig could have ended in disaster.

It happened at a giant sports arena in Los Angeles when Bono entered the crowd carrying a flag. Correctly gauging the intensity of an overwrought audience's collective emotions can be extremely difficult. This time it turned out to be overwhelming.

Hemmed in on all sides, Bono had been swept willy-nilly off the floor of the arena and upstairs, into the balcony. The flag, meanwhile, had been wrenched from his grasp and frenziedly ripped apart. It was all happening bewilderingly fast. His clothes were rapidly going the same way as the flag. And the suffocating mixture of emotions had spilled over for one young man, with whom suddenly Bono found himself in a confrontational situation.

Backing away from this, Bono thought to restore some sense by threatening to jump off the balcony if the situation did not calm down. The next moment, he had jumped. The fans, 20 feet below, delightedly caught their idol and lowered him to his feet. Bono nearly naked, his tattered clothes hanging from him, returned as quickly as he could to the stage. But, caught up in the madness, other fans on the balcony were by now likewise diving off. Fortunately, they too all found soft landings but the horror of what might have been crashed in on Bono immediately.

Backstage after the gig ended, he was paralysed with remorse about what his actions, however inadvertent, might have caused to happen. The other three, witnessing the whole thing from the stage, had been equally horrified. They were unanimous when they told Bono, 'We have got to stop this, right now.'

He did not need to be told. Already appalled, his responsibility was bearing down on him strongly, and he has since openly described his behaviour that night as having been 'disgraceful'. Edge later commented on this madness, saying, 'I felt it undermined the dignity and nobility of the music.'

The weeks on the road would also throw up other kinds of passion. Bono, Larry Mullen and Edge maintained their Christian faith in their own way. They were not regular churchgoers and, as they preferred to meet in private prayer sessions, this was something that being constantly on the move did not need to hinder. Occasionally Bono would read the Bible while travelling between cities.

Though he was free with the press about almost anything, Bono was still reluctant to discuss his religious beliefs in public in any depth. This area should, he reiterated, be a private matter. It followed then that he would dislike the popular American television evangelists whom he viewed as being avaricious.

More than that, these flashy, self-styled preachers made him see red. His powerful gut instinct, he admitted, on seeing these razzmatazz shows, was to toss the television set out of the hotel window. And, although he resisted the temptation to do so, he felt deeply aggrieved by what he saw as the commercialization of religious faith. Incensed, he declared, 'I believe it is tarnishing something really beautiful.'

After their rollercoaster experience in the States, in June U2 arrived back in the more tranquil environment of Ireland for a well-earned rest. For Larry Mullen, Adam Clayton and Edge, this still meant returning to their respective parents' homes. For Bono, home with Ali remained the beachfront cottage near Howth.

For the first few weeks after his return Bono had some difficulty unwinding. His body clock was still geared up mid-evening, as if he was about to take the stage. This made him pumped up and very restless.

Home life, though, was precious to Bono. Ali alone understood the paradoxical nature of his personality – a personality that enabled him to be boldly extrovert, but then on other rare occasions to be so introverted that he would have to force himself to enter a room full of people. And those vulnerable periods, when Bono suffered a mental block when writing songs, were times when he also counted on his wife to urge him through to the other side.

In a broader sense he was content to call Dublin home and he was happy that it remained the band's base. Its people, although appreciative of talent, nevertheless remain resolutely unimpressed by the trappings of success; an attitude that Bono found refreshing. He once remarked that he believed it was healthy for rock stars to metaphorically receive a slap down every so often, just to keep life in perspective, and that Dublin was the place to get that.

To illustrate this Bono will, tongue-in-cheek, remark that in the United States people look at the successful man in the mansion on the hill and say, 'One day, I'm gonna be like him.' Whereas, in Dublin some people are more likely to look at the man in the mansion and say, 'One day, I'm gonna get that bastard.' Like the rest of U2, Bono had no intention of decamping to London at the first hint of fame. Musically, his ambitions were clear. He envisioned stretching U2's capabilities to the extreme, while finding a way of blending aggressive stimulation with palpable sensitivity.

For U2 the stimulation of performing again came when, mid August 1983, they headlined at an open-air rock festival held at

Dublin's Phoenix Park. Other participating acts included Big Country, Eurythmics and Simple Minds. Fresh from their successful United States tour, U2 gave a blistering performance, thrilling the 20,000 plus crowd. The audience added a personal touch to proceedings when, with a little prompting, they serenaded Edge with 'Happy Birthday' in honour of him having lately turned twenty-two.

As the echoing cries for encores faded away and people filtered off into the night, there was a tangible awareness among the band of having reached the end of the first phase. And that vivid sensation tied in with Bono's expressed belief that *War* had marked a watershed moment for U2. He maintained that a weight had now been lifted off their shoulders and that they were free to start afresh.

Part of this fresh beginning would bring with it a new challenge before the year's end. But, before that, November saw the release of U2's first live album. Called *Under a Blood Red Sky*, its tracks having been recorded at various American and West German gigs, it captured the electric atmosphere of U2's live performances.

With Jimmy Iovine producing, it was the first album that the band had made without Steve Lillywhite. Lillywhite had a self-imposed rule of not producing more than two albums with any band. He had already broken that rule with U2 – *War* had made it three. And so this time, by mutual agreement, they had had to consider bringing in new blood.

The eight-song mini album *Under a Blood Red Sky* did not quite emulate *War*'s chart-topping performance, but it did secure the number two slot in Britain and eventually reached number twenty-eight in America.

Chart success in Britain added welcome impetus to the prospect of embarking on their first tour of the Far East. Since the 1970s, Japan had become a fertile hunting ground for western rock groups and U2 kicked off their short engagement there in Osaka, and ended it with a raft of gigs in Tokyo. Then it was back to London to take part in a peace benefit gig called 'The Big One', held at the Apollo Theatre.

After this appearance U2 called a halt to global junketing and retreated behind closed doors for much of the first six months of 1984. Their intended fresh start would not just happen on its own. Bono needed peace, as did the others. They wanted to re-evaluate their position in terms of songwriting, although their core principles would always remain the same.

Manager Paul McGuinness later reflected that there were times when it might well have made commercial sense for U2 to churn out a hit single in a tried and trusted vein, to avoid the risk of being overtaken and forgotten in an overcrowded and competitive industry. But no one in the band, its management or the record company wanted them to sacrifice their integrity and Bono had no intention of capitulating for the sake of an easy cash-in.

U2 wanted to be successful but, uniquely, they were not *obsessed* with rampant commercial success. They wanted it on their own terms, and attaining their creative goals was always their primary objective. Edge stressed, around this time, that all four preferred to focus on the 'journey', and evaluate what they had experienced on the way, rather than just the end product. This year then would see the release of just one U2 single in the UK from the new album, and these releases were slated for late in 1984.

To help their 'reincarnation', the band wanted to get out of the sterile environment of the studio. In their search for an alternative recording venue they eventually settled on Slane Castle. Situated 20 miles north of Dublin in County Meath, this imposing pile is the property of Lord Henry Mountcharles.

This would be their first album since renewing their contract with Island Records. The original plan was to lay down the basic tracks at the castle, then to carry out the overdubbing work at Windmill Lane Studios, where they would also mix the album. Bono joined his bandmates at Slane Castle throughout the summer but all did not go like clockwork, and by September they would still be sculpting the material.

At Slane Castle they operated mainly in the ballroom and in the library. Although they had been made welcome there, it is hardly surprising that things took a while to knit together satisfactorily. The strangeness of new surroundings – even if they eventually prove to be stimulating – can initially have an inhibiting effect. They were aiming, too, in an experimental direction. And, to cap it all, the band had engaged the services of not one but two producers, neither of whom they had worked with before, which meant that there was a degree of settling in to be accommodated on both sides.

One of the producers was Brian Eno, the Suffolk-born composer and keyboard player who had been a founder member of the stylish 1970s band Roxy Music. Eno was unfamiliar with U2's work to date but the band was already aware of him as a performer in his own right. When the four had bounced the names of possible producers around, that of Brian Eno had surfaced more often than any other.

When they eventually linked up with Eno, he in turn took on board his regular collaborator, Canadian engineer Daniel Lanois. Together, all six found a good rapport though. Once the glitches were ironed out, they would eventually, after some re-recording, produce U2's warmest album yet.

Lyrically, Bono's maturing ability was raising the stakes. His grasp of language was now even further enhanced, allowing him to create a rich tapestry of images in song. A few, particularly powerful tracks were destined to stand out. 'Bad' had been written after Bono witnessed the traumatic battle some friends had fought with heroin addiction in Dublin. And two numbers, 'MLK' and 'Pride', were in memory of the murdered civil rights leader Martin Luther King.

'Pride' – a soaring tribute, reportedly written in an incredible seven minutes – fitted with U2's socio-political stance and Bono invested enormous passion in the number. During the recording session he gave it the works, windmilling his arms above his head, wringing every drop of emotion out of himself. When the producers

above: Having formed while still at school, U2 are one of the very few globally successful rock bands whose personnel has remained steadfastly unchanged for over two decades.

right: Bono's fresh-faced youth-fulness and his mischievous streak blended intriguingly with his deeply insightful songwriting and his propensity to be outspoken on any number of serious world issues.

above: Stylewise Bono has changed a lot over the years, but by the mid 1980s he had already become a potently powerful figure in rock music.

below: Famous in the early 1990s for his motley cast of bizarre stage characters, probably Bono's most theatrical incarnation was the gaudy, seedy and devilish MacPhisto.

and others gently teased him about it afterwards, he became somewhat defensive. He had been, throughout, fully aware of the uplifting experience, however, and described feeling as if he had been ten feet tall.

The album would be called *The Unforgettable Fire* – a title inspired by a collection of paintings and exhibits which the band had viewed during their recent tour of Japan, the work of survivors of the atomic bombs that were dropped at Hiroshima and Nagasaki. Finishing touches were made to the album for an autumn release and attention could turn to other recent developments.

Earlier in the summer, Bono had stepped outside U2 to make a guest appearance when in July, near Dublin, he had duetted with the legendary Bob Dylan. Dylan asked Bono to sing with him on the number 'Leopardskin Pill-Box Hat' from his critically worshipped 1966 album *Blonde On Blonde*. Bono agreed, despite not knowing the lyrics. Consequently, what should have been a very special moment was, for Bono, a shambles, and a potentially offensive fiasco for Dylan.

Once off-stage as the show continued, Bono believed that he had well and truly blown it. But a little later he received an invitation to rejoin Dylan at the end of the gig for a rendition of the more universally known standard 'Blowin' in the Wind'.

Bono was on stage like a flash but confusion quickly reigned once again, when he sang in a different key and seemed to have added supplementary words to this much-loved classic, thereby throwing Dylan clean off his stride. Newspaper critics next day slaughtered Bono; he also personally received a few frank homegrown verbal reviews from passersby in the street. But Bono had meant no disrespect to Bob Dylan.

The then 43-year-old American singer/songwriter had influenced a generation and had inspired many to enter the music world. U2, with their recording future now secure, still remained fully aware of how hard it was for bands, especially Irish bands, to gain a foothold in the business. So in August 1984 they set up Mother Records. The prime function of this company was to help young talented unknowns to get started by affording them advice about the pitfalls in the music business, as well as providing access to professional facilities to make high-quality demos. With these, they could, hopefully, go out and impress established major record labels.

That done, U2 got back to nurturing their own career. This month they also launched a new series of tours which would take them around the globe. The first stop was Australia and New Zealand. From where, at the end of September, they propelled themselves once again through Europe. 'Pride (In the Name of Love)'/'Boomerang' had been released on 15 September and had risen to number three in the British charts.

Pleasure at this latest success helped to lift their spirits as, in late October, having traversed the Netherlands, Scandinavia, Germany and Italy, they arrived in France for a clutch of dates culminating in Paris.

They had been playing across France in a succession of large marquees in unreliable weather. And by the time they hit the French capital, rain began to plague them. At one point the rain leaking through the canvas and dripping onto the instruments made the keyboards pack in. And the press of bodies squeezed inside the large canvas produced an unpleasant heat that created condensation.

Bono nevertheless gave a high-energy performance in what was altogether a strong show. One of the most unusual moments came when they performed a number called 'The Electric Company'.

Like many of U2's lyrics, the song had a deeper meaning than one might first assume. It described the electric shock treatment endured by a friend of the band's who, as a patient in a mental hospital, suffered from the delusion that he was Jesus; the ECT treatment was meant to cure him. To illustrate the physical torment inflicted by this treatment, Bono acted out the grotesque twitching and jolting reflexes of a human body receiving an electric charge. If it took some members of the audience some time to figure out what was actually going on, it nevertheless left an indelible impression.

On a lighter note, as U2 headed to London in late October in anticipation of the start of the British leg of their tour, *The Unforgettable Fire* was released. Dubbed 'a moody, almost mystical album' by *Hot Press*, it replicated *War*'s achievement by entering the UK album charts at the top.

Riding on the crest of a wave, U2 trekked the now familiar route around England with a brief early foray north of the border, this time only as far as Edinburgh and Glasgow, before returning to London.

After that, with barely time to draw breath, they took the tour on to the States, where the new album would better the performance of 'Pride' (which had stalled at number thirty-three in the US singles charts) by reaching number twelve. The US leg of the tour ended in mid-December and Bono was home for Christmas.

The American excursion had been crowned by *Rolling Stone* magazine heralding U2 as being 'the band that matters'. And looking back over the year, there were rewarding moments to reflect on in terms of the band's growth and, for Bono, in terms also of his personal fulfilment. One event, however, stood out. That was when during the British tour Bono had taken time out to participate in what became a historic recording.

In early November 1984 Boomtown Rats' singer Bob Geldof had been deeply moved by a special BBC television news report on the tragic human consequences of a devastating famine in Ethiopia. Inspired to do something, he hatched an ambitious plan to produce an all-star charity single, from which no one involved would take any profit.

It was arranged super-fast and, within two weeks, thirty-six invited established rock artistes turned up on 25 November at Sarm Studios in London's Notting Hill to record a song called 'Do They

Know It's Christmas?'. It had been co-written by Bob Geldof and ex-Ultravox singer, Midge Ure.

Under the banner name of Band Aid, among the artistes taking part were Cliff Richard, Sting, Boy George, Annie Lennox, Francis Rossi, Rick Parfitt, Paul Weller, Phil Collins, George Michael and Paul Young. Adam Clayton lent his bass skills and Bono contributed one of the unmistakable lead vocal parts.

'Do They Know It's Christmas?' became the 1984 number one Christmas single. Moreover, it raised millions of pounds for the famine relief and the song became the biggest selling single ever in Britain for the next thirteen years. For Bono, it was one of many future charitable acts. His humanitarian efforts had not yet properly begun.

CHAPTER 6

Humanitarian

WITH SALES OF *The Unforgettable Fire* passing the one million mark, sold-out European tours bookended U2's most successful onslaught yet on America in spring 1985. The US leg reached its crescendo in April with a headlining performance at the prestigious Madison Square Garden in New York City.

Rolling Stone magazine now honoured U2 with the title 'The Band of the Eighties'. Although, with half of the decade still to go, it seemed a somewhat premature pronouncement, it was true that Bono, Adam Clayton, Larry Mullen and Edge had all grown enormously in stature. They could now bestride the world's best venue stages with complete confidence.

Their unshaken poise during the ninety-minute set at the Garden completely won over the 20,000 capacity crowd. Many fans held burning cigarette lighters above their heads – a forest of individual flames that signified a universal approval.

Surefooted throughout, Bono kept control of the night. When some fans passed the Irish tricolour up to him during 'Sunday Bloody Sunday', he obligingly hung it on the mike stand. But he then promptly covered it with a white flag. As well as symbolizing the spirit of reconciliation, this was also aimed at diluting any potentially inflammatory connotations.

He found no difficulty either in defusing the situation when a couple of worked-up fans rushed on to the stage. Instead of retreating to a safe place and allowing the enthusiastic stage security to summarily eject the intruders, Bono greeted the two with disarming friendliness. After speaking to them amiably for a short while, he talked them into leaving the stage voluntarily.

For another young man, the night ended on a magical note. During the encore Bono extended a general open invitation for a guitar player from the audience to join the band on stage. One normally shy guy cast aside his inhibitions and duly clambered up.

Bono placed his own acoustic guitar in the fan's hands and showed him the four basic chords that would allow the youth to accompany U2 on the Bob Dylan song 'Knockin' on Heaven's Door'. When it came to the time to jam, the overwhelmed youngster performed with perhaps more haste than grace, but he would live on the memory of having done so for a long time to come.

All bands consider playing at Madison Square Garden to be major league stuff. Thin Lizzy's lead guitarist Scott Gorham states, 'The building ain't much in itself, but you know you're there. It's Madison Square Garden – you've made it!' And U2 had indeed begun their elevation into a higher echelon than that reached by most of their contemporaries.

The old adage that it is possible to gauge quite a lot about a person's character from their record collection has always held true. But in the mid-1980s there were still only a select number of bands with which people were proud to be openly identified.

It had begun in the swinging sixties when it became a badge of faith to be either a Beatles fan, or a Rolling Stones freak; the choice to be the latter meant that your rebellious spirit was stamped invisibly on your forehead. Likewise, in the same era, to be a Bob Dylan devotee indicated that you were an intellectual type, a philosopher of the human condition.

By now people felt that supporting U2 definitely said something about themselves. U2 stood for certain ideals and their fans had particular expectations of them that went far beyond the usual hero-worship bargain.

Their supporters looked to U2 never to stand still. The band ought to maintain all its hallmarks of honesty and integrity and should hold fast to particular principles. Yet at the same time, they were to be constantly innovative.

For his part, Bono had lately come to believe that, since their recording debut five years earlier, they had at last formed a unique nucleus that would be forever special. And he had no doubt about what lay at its core. 'It's the songs we serve. That is our complete goal,' he said.

That said, being four good-looking young rock stars they also attracted their traditional fair share of uncomplicated adoring female hearts. At Madison Square Garden, though, Bono dismayed many of his female fans when he clearly dedicated the song 'A Sort of Homecoming' to his wife Ali, who was in the audience that night, with the words, 'To the one I love.'

Unlike most rock frontmen, certainly those in their twenties, Bono had never set himself up as an object of attainable desire. By romantically acknowledging his wife in this way he signalled openly that he would not play that particular game.

Yet he missed the close personal contact he'd once had with the band's supporters. It bothered him that people now increasingly approached him either with star-struck tongue-tied reserve, or with starry-eyed gushing fervour. Too often these encounters lost any vestige of naturalness, which disappointed him.

More and more often, as a result of this, instead of socializing in public, he joined the ranks of so many in his position and remained marooned in the sanctuary of his hotel room. Referring to the mind-numbing boredom that sets in when this experience is repeated nightly for months on end on consecutive tours, Bono once declared, 'I can understand how a lot of people get into drugs.'

The reason why he personally did not succumb to this temptation, he put down to having many positive forces in his life to keep him interested. He would refute, however, the growing perception of him as an invincibly strong-willed man. Instead he admitted to being all too aware of his weaknesses.

Bono was not alone in refusing to slip into the sewer of drug addiction. He later highlighted how many pressures there had been for the whole band precisely because they *did* avoid this almost obligatory pitfall when he stated, 'We almost felt that we *should* do drugs out of guilt, to make people feel at home.'

U2's extraordinarily blameless lifestyle, together with their known association with Christian beliefs, meant that the music press had started to typecast them as holier-than-thou, and brand Bono as a kind of Mr Clean. But that was too harsh. Puritanical they were not, as was demonstrated during the making of *The Unforgettable Fire*.

Eccentrically they had held what they called a 'naked day' when those involved in the recording and production sessions for this album did so in the nude. Apparently, some individuals chose to have fun with rolls of thick, black, industrial adhesive tape; mischief that later induced some eye-watering consequences when it came to removing the tape.

On the same day as the American tour ended – 4 May – the new single 'The Unforgettable Fire'/'A Sort of Homecoming' was released in Britain, where it peaked a week later at number six. And, as U2 prepared to embark on their second European tour of the year, which would take them into early June, Bono reflected on the band's approach to music now, in contrast to when they were starting out.

This year, 1985, had marked a deliberate departure from the battle-cry style of old and there had been a conscious softening of tone. As such, it demanded a more subtle, internal performance than Bono's natural on-stage exuberance normally gave rise to.

Bono still believed in the importance of what the band was saying. But he no longer felt the need to be so uptight about everything. He now recognized the fusion of fear and tension that had been prevalent in his voice before, and he acknowledged, too, how uncomfortably preachy he might have appeared to some people in the past.

It was in his voice that Bono registered one of the first rewards of this new lessening of tension, for by relaxing, he had – he believed – become a singer once more on *The Unforgettable Fire*.

In the studio sessions for this album Bono's favourite sounding board had become Adam Clayton, whose instincts proved to be a valuable barometer of the strength of the work in progress. The bass player also seemed to viscerally understand where Bono should be and where he wanted to go. Consequently they had enjoyed developing a closer working relationship.

Despite the album's success, not every track found favour and one track in particular – 'Elvis Presley and America' – provoked much comment. Bono readily conceded that the song could bamboozle a lot of people. But some Presley fans were downright riled by it.

Bono considers the American legend to have been a genius. Equally he had been saddened by Elvis's decline towards a premature sudden death at the age of forty-two in 1977. Before this he had battled against the effects of excessive indulgence in prescribed medication – effects which had at times been all too painfully obvious in some of his latter stage appearances. It was primarily this final phase of Elvis Presley's extraordinary life that Bono had had in mind when he had crafted the first outline of the song.

Bono admitted that it was a rougher-than-usual, spontaneous composition but he also believed it to be an evocative piece of work. Initially, he had hesitated about including the number in the album but in the end he had been persuaded to allow it. Furthermore, he had been encouraged to leave the track in its original raw state. Although some listeners would question the wisdom of this, in the spirit of loosening up Bono eventually decided that it had been right to do so.

The new approach to recording also signalled a fresh approach to touring – hence the more internal performances. However, there were some teething problems when they first put theory into practice. And by the time the European tour passed through Germany in May 1985 they had had to abandon the idea. The band had become so rudderless that a frisson of danger lurked nightly on stage.

Nevertheless, their passion for performing remained intact. And, as self-confessed adrenalin addicts, all four responded to this extra, if unplanned, edge, while at the same time subtly altering the way in which they played. The main thrust was to get the audience actually listening to the music, absorbing more with their ears rather than just being visually captivated.

Having successfully topped the bill on 22 June at the Milton Keynes Bowl in Britain, exactly one week later U2 made their first live stage appearance in Ireland for two years. It was at Dublin's Croke Park, before a 55,000 strong crowd and it had been anticipated in the Irish press as being a magnificent homecoming for the lads.

There was a particular resonance at one point during this gig when it came to their rendition of 'Sunday Bloody Sunday'. In addition to the 1972 incident in Londonderry, the original 'Bloody Sunday' had occurred sixty-five years previously, on 21 November 1920. In retaliation for the killing earlier in the day of fourteen British officers and officials, the Black and Tans (members of the British armed forces sent to Ireland in the 1920s) had descended on the Gaelic Athletic Association's headquarters just before a football match and gunfire had rung out.

Twelve people died, some having been shot, and some having been crushed to death by the terrified, stampeding crowd. The football match had been *at* Croke Park.

Coming from a country so steeped in what traditionally binds as well as divides its people, U2 would certainly have been aware of the venue's significance. But for their part, they were just pleased to have chalked up the latest in a string of triumphant live performances.

The downside for Bono was that he had, by now, developed serious trouble in getting to sleep at night after performing at these giant outdoor gigs. To help combat this insomnia he took to drinking – by his usually moderate standards – copious amounts of wine. This contributed to a tendency that started around now to drink too much in general.

Perhaps it was inevitable. As was the fact that, due to U2's heavy touring schedules, come summer 1985 the stage had become more familiar to Bono than his own home. He grimly joked, 'Home is where the carpet is' (referring to the stretch of carpeting that the band's stage-hands carted around from city to city for each gig). But the truth was that Bono was better acquainted with the paraphernalia of performing than with the furniture in the home he shared with Ali, to the extent that he once even declared, 'I do not have a home.'

The nomadic existence that had begun in January was actually drawing to a close and would climax in style with an appearance at London's Wembley Stadium on 13 July 1985. The event was called Live Aid and, like Band Aid, it was the brainchild of Bob Geldof and Midge Ure.

Live Aid was a truly historic event: a sixteen-hour marathon gig that kicked off at noon at Wembley Stadium. By 6 p.m. British time the transmitters had hooked up by satellite to a parallel gig at the JFK Stadium in Philadelphia, USA. And the event was ultimately broadcast live to over a billion people worldwide.

Among the artistes taking part were Queen, Bob Dylan, Elton John, Status Quo, Tina Turner, Bryan Adams, David Bowie, Dire Straits, Mick Jagger and Paul McCartney and each act had been allocated a slot of roughly twenty minutes.

Logistically, it was a gargantuan undertaking, one that required state-of-the-art equipment. This included a revolving stage split into three segments – one for the band in performance, one for the next band to set up their equipment, and one for the band just finished playing to dismantle their gear.

After a damp, dreary week the sun made a guest appearance on the Saturday for the crowds (some of whom had camped out overnight on the cold stone pavements). They flocked into Wembley Stadium, where at midday Status Quo launched into their appropriately titled 1977 belter 'Rockin' All Over the World'.

There was an electric awareness among the crowd of taking part in something special and this feeling intensified as the day unfolded, with one top performer after another streaming on and off stage.

The event had also captured U2's imagination. Bono, sensitive to the fundamental impulse behind what was being dubbed 'a global jukebox', took time out backstage to quietly pray, before U2 was introduced via satellite from America by actor Jack Nicholson.

Led by Freddie Mercury, who gave one of his most dynamic performances, Queen was universally considered to have been the best band on the day. But many other bands also turned in first-rate performances, among them U2. Bono's vocal range had been steadily developing and the 25-year-old's once youthful yearning tones had now matured into a gravelly roar.

Given the time restriction, it made sense to perform their best-loved numbers. Bono also provided a memorable moment when, during one song, he climbed down into the sectioned-off security area to dance with a young girl who had breathlessly broken through the cordon to be near her hero.

Although each performer took part in Live Aid for the right charitable reasons, it was an obvious by-product of such massive exposure that individual profiles would be raised, flagging popularity restored, and even jaded palates whetted once more. And naturally, it turned a whole new generation of fans on to particular groups.

The *raison d'être* of the event had never been to give rock stars a global platform to promote themselves, but commercially some artistes certainly ended up benefiting greatly from their brief stint in the spotlight at Live Aid. That U2 was one of the bands to benefit in this way disturbed Bono.

A recent EP 'Wide Awake in America', whose four tracks were 'Bad'/'A Sort of Homecoming (live)'/'The Three Sunrises'/'Love Comes Tumbling', had been released in May in America only, where it had quickly stalled at number thirty-seven. But within a fortnight of Live Aid, enough copies had been imported into Britain for the EP to reach number eleven.

As it happened, summer 1985 had been the point anyway at which, according to Bono, U2 had at last begun to make substantial money. He made no claims to being a millionaire, dollar or otherwise. And his attitude to money was, in any case, somewhat unusual.

The days when U2 had struggled financially were not so distant that Bono had forgotten the band appearing on the influential BBC television programme *Top of the Pops* for the second time, only to have to wend their way back home to Ireland by bus afterwards to save cash. He also candidly speculated that, behind the glitzy facade of pop music, the harsh reality was that there could not be many artistes with actual money in the bank, sufficient money – that is – to live on for life.

Naturally it was in everyone's interest that U2 prospered financially and every band member was aware of the steps being taken to ensure that this happened. Although Bono was adamant that his life was rich before he ever had a lot of money, he was not so sentimental as to claim that money did not matter.

On the contrary, he was acutely aware that, considering the desperate plight of the starving millions in the Sudan, it would be grossly insensitive to dismiss the importance of being well off. What concerned him was that the increased accumulation of wealth might come to constitute a threat to the integrity of the band. He was anxious that their focus should remain clear.

It was to regain his own personal focus that he went to Ethiopia in September. In part it was due to his uneasiness at U2 benefiting commercially from their participation in the historic Live Aid gig. But he also had a strong need to see the situation out there for himself, and to offer practical help in the famine relief effort. He was accompanied by Ali and they would stay for a month.

They wanted no publicity and Bono later stressed that he sought no plaudits for having taking a trip that he could afford to take. Instead, he insisted that it was the unsung anonymous aid workers who tirelessly worked out in Ethiopia who were worthy of respect.

Bono and Ali joined some volunteers who worked in one of the feeding stations, a fenced-in and guarded compound that Bono later described as resembling a wartime concentration camp. Only the grim fortifications were not designed to keep people confined, but to safeguard food and medical supplies that would be distributed to the masses outside the perimeter wire.

Sharing a tent by night, the couple got involved in the everyday chores of running a refugee camp, with Bono rolling up his sleeves and getting stuck into manual labour, sometimes literally shovelling dirt.

Cleanliness and personal hygiene, as well as an understanding of good nutrition, were also vital in winning the war against the spread of disease. So, while they were there, Bono and Ali worked on writing a few simple songs and playlets on these subjects. Once translated into their native language, these could be taught to the people in a way that would educate them in an entertaining fashion and that would pass on essential information that would hopefully linger in their minds.

Every day, work started early and went on till late in an effort to help the throng of emaciated spectral figures; the aid workers daily facing indescribably agonizing life-and-death choices.

Now sporting a moustache and beard, and with hair as long as his darkly beautiful wife's, Bono took on a native look. While confronting the depths of this human suffering, he was horribly aware that he and Ali were two very small cogs in a vast and relentless wheel. It was perhaps not surprising that soon afterwards he confessed, 'I felt more removed from Christianity, not what it is but what it has become.'

There is no doubt that the experience etched itself deeply on Bono's consciousness. Once home, he found that the enduring spirit of the Ethiopian people in their desperate battle to stay alive contrasted rudely with the naked selfishness that seemed all too prevalent in the developed world.

Emotionally raw, the month working side by side had created a particularly intense bond between Bono and Ali. However, the fact that he had spent most of the year prior to this trip on the road, consolidating the success of *The Unforgettable Fire* and meeting other professional demands, was about to start placing a degree of strain on his personal life.

Professionally, too, this was to be another period of introspection. Entering the last quarter of 1985, Bono believed that U2 had, in a sense, only now completed its apprenticeship. The hard core of fans who had followed them since the late 1970s may have taken issue with that. But Bono also owned up to how much he had always feared being a songwriter, admitting that it was only at this point that he had 'come to terms' with the role.

In fact Bono had always appeared to be a natural communicator. Certainly holding back had never been his style, either inside or outside his music. And now his commitment to a growing catalogue of causes was set to grow, thereby placing new platforms before him.

Having idolized the late Martin Luther King, Bono had already joined the anti-apartheid lobby in America, taking part in protest marches against the then South African regime. As a result, U2 had received a personal message of thanks for their support from the prominent South African religious leader Archbishop Desmond Tutu.

In November Bono lent his vocals to a single called 'Sun City', recorded under the banner name of Artistes United Against Apartheid, which peaked at number twenty-one in Britain and number thirty-eight in America. He also guested on the track 'Silver and Gold' on the parent album.

In addition, Amnesty International, the non-profit-making Human Rights organization to whom U2 already contributed money, had confirmed that U2 would be taking part in one of a series of benefit gigs to commemorate Amnesty International's twenty-fifth anniversary in summer 1986.

The band's and Bono's increased identification with environmental and social causes also began to attract some words of caution. Some believed they should not try to shoulder too many of the world's problems, and thereby risk a burn-out. Who guitarist Pete Townshend was one of those voices. He said specifically of the tireless frontman, 'What Bono has to realize pretty quick is that no one man can do it all.'

U2's charitable endeavours would continue in the coming months but 1986 also dawned with recognition from within the music industry when one rock magazine readers' poll voted them as 'Band of the Year', and live gigs loomed large.

Of these gigs, the notably altruistic endeavours included firstly U2 taking part on 17 May in a live all-day event held in Dublin called Self Aid. Here they joined Van Morrison and the Pogues, among other rock acts, to raise money for the long-term unemployed in Ireland.

By the mid-1980s unemployment had become chronic and morale was desperately low. Britain now staggered under Margaret Thatcher's Conservative regime and the outlook was just as bleak in Dublin.

U2's set at Self Aid included the Bob Dylan song 'Maggie's

Farm' and Bono, attuned to the underlying anger felt by many, astutely articulated that rage and directed it at the politicians who sat in their ivory towers, far removed from the hopeless wasteland their policies created.

Bono and the band were soon accused of political naivety. And they themselves queried the ultimate effectiveness of the event in terms of producing real results. But at the time their participation had been well intentioned.

Within weeks, on 4 June 1986, U2, now in America, took part as promised in Amnesty International's silver anniversary celebration charity tour, dubbed 'A Conspiracy of Hope'. With guest performers also including Sting, Lou Reed, Bryan Adams and Peter Gabriel, the tour saw six shows played in different arenas and stadia stretching from San Francisco on California's West Coast, to East Rutherford in New Jersey in the East, and every one was sold out. U2's appearance took place at San Francisco's gigantic Cow Palace.

Bono once remarked that at these kinds of gigs, audiences had a tendency to think that simply by them attending on the night, the problem – whatever it was – had been sorted. Fortunately the upshot of Amnesty International's high-profile tour – which had aimed to raise US$1 million – besides succeeding in raising substantial funds, was also that the organization's membership had tripled by the tour's end on 15 June.

The success of the tour pleased U2 but little over a fortnight later the band, and in particular Bono, received a severe body blow. At the start of July 1986 one of his best friends, Greg Carroll, was killed when the motorcycle he was riding was in collision with a car in Dublin.

The twenty-six-year-old had met U2 when the band had played in Auckland, New Zealand, a couple of years earlier during *The Unforgettable Fire* tour Down Under. They had struck up an instant rapport, to the point that Greg Carroll had come on staff as a crew member, and had subsequently moved over to live in Dublin.

Bono described Greg as having been like a brother, revealing how Carroll had often escorted Ali socially in his absence, to keep her company. Greg Carroll had also looked after Bono's Harley Davidson motorbike, though he had not been riding it on the night of the fatal accident.

Shattered by the death, Bono along with Larry Mullen attended Greg's funeral which was held in New Zealand; Bono also penned the song 'One Tree Hill' as a moving memorial to his dead friend. This sudden death made Bono so aware of the fragility of human life that, for a long time afterwards, whenever the telephone rang, his heart would momentarily freeze in dread of hearing more bad news.

It is fair to say that that summer Bono went through some personal turmoil. He later admitted to having got into the habit again of drinking too much. On occasions this over-indulgence was partly a rejection of his burgeoning saintly image, which in itself indicated a potential crisis of identity.

A foreign trip which he undertook with Ali might have helped take his mind off his grief, had the trip not turned out to be a memorable experience for all the wrong reasons.

It was never meant to be a relaxing vacation. Rather, it was intended to be more of a fact-finding mission. Abuse of human rights in all forms concerned the singer and his focus had zeroed in on El Salvador, in Central America, which right then was one of the world's trouble hot spots.

The El Salvador government was fighting a socialist guerilla movement. US foreign policy at this time, under President Ronald Reagan, meant that American troops had become involved in El Salvador in an effort to aid the government there, in their battle against the socialists. It was a foreign policy that U2 would later speak out against, but at that point Bono's thoughts ran in a more personal vein.

He had previously taken an interest in the establishing of some communes there, and he had acquaintances near the country's capital, San Salvador. Worryingly, Bono had recently learned that some people in that region were being summarily rounded up and imprisoned, and he had decided to travel to San Salvador to witness the situation first hand. Bono and Ali, who was equally determined to go, knew in advance that they could be walking into danger with this trip. But nothing prepared Bono for his own reaction.

They arrived in San Salvador at the height of the fighting and headed out into the countryside, towards one of the villages situated in the surrounding hills. Before they got to their destination though, the village came under attack from mortar fire.

As bombs exploded and fighter planes roared aggressively overhead, like the rest of his companions, Bono's first instinct was to run and take cover. Only in the open ground there was no cover. Panicked, and afraid for Ali as well as himself, it hardly registered with him at first when a local peasant farmer who had been working the land nearby tried in his imperfect English to calm his fears. The man pointed out that, alarming though the sound of the explosions was, the danger lay some distance away, in and around the village, and not where the party of travellers had come to a paralysed halt.

The man's kindly reassurance eventually sunk in and restored sanity, only for Bono in practically the next instant to experience a mixture of feelings – none of them good. First he felt a fool for having panicked. Then he felt humble that the local farmer's unruffled response indicated more clearly than anything else could have, just how commonplace this kind of mortar attack was in his everyday life. Most of all, Bono would never forget the undiluted fear that he had felt in those first few moments.

And this was not their only ordeal. During this trip Bono and his companions also had the misfortune to cross the path of a small band of trigger-happy troops who menacingly let rip with a burst of machine-gun fire over the tops of the travellers' heads. This time Bono knew it was just a warning, intended only to shake them up. But it still, by his own admission, made him feel physically sick.

All things considered, it is understandable that Bono would look back on 1986 as, personally, having been a bad year. Particularly when, added to all that had happened, was the fact that he had not spent much time with his wife over the twelve months and that was taking its toll too.

Although the Hewsons are a couple who guard their personal privacy strictly, Bono openly admitted that he and Ali experienced some problems around now due to the stress of him being unable to devote sufficient time to their marriage because of the demanding rise in the band's commitments. His comment on how this marital tension crystallized was to admit to having been thrown out of their home on a few occasions by his strong-minded wife. Years later, though, still married and with an expanding family, this situation would clearly resolve itself.

Within the band, too, another kind of relationship was gradually improving. Because Adam Clayton had remained separate from his band mates when it came to practising their religious beliefs, the bass player had (only in this particular respect) been portrayed in the press as being the odd man out in U2.

Clayton himself has acknowledged that until late 1986 he had been in a sort of wilderness. The by-product of this had sometimes been a noticeable air of antagonism within the band.

In virtually any other rock outfit, Adam Clayton's lifestyle – that of a young, successful, bachelor rock star – would have been completely normal. It was when it was contrasted with the behaviour of the rest of U2 (as Clayton put it, 'clean living people') that he stood out. Now, however, because the other three could see his way of life as Clayton establishing his own identity, any past tensions were evaporating.

So it was in this new, thawed-out atmosphere that the business at hand started up all over again for U2. By August 1986 Bono had rejoined the others in their Dublin studios to commence work on their next album, once again with producers Brian Eno and Daniel Lanois.

There had been no U2 record release in Britain all year but the material they would produce in the coming months – although as yet unwritten – was destined to catapult U2 into a different league altogether.

CHAPTER 7

Idol

I T HAD SURPRISED MANY that, despite U2's impressive reputation as a live act, a number one album or single in America had
continued to elude them. This deficit, though, vanished with
the arrival – on 21 March 1987 – of *The Joshua Tree*.

Universally considered to be a masterpiece, and for many still
the band's career high spot, the album entered the UK charts at
the top and reached the same position across the Atlantic a month
later.

Exactly one week after the British release of the album, came the
scorching ballad 'With Or Without You', backed by 'Luminous
Times (Hold On to Love)'. While peaking at number four in the
domestic market, by mid-May it had notched up U2's first number
one in the American singles' chart.

This sudden Stateside sweep coincided with the launch of a
mammoth world tour that had commenced in Arizona on 2 April
and would bring them, during the six-week countrywide trek, a
plethora of praise. It was at this point that U2 became only the third
rock band to feature on the cover of *Time* magazine. (The Beatles
and the Who were the other two bands.)

The headline hollered, 'U2: Rock's Hottest Ticket'. And by now, along with the rest of the band, Bono knew that *The Joshua Tree*, by dint of having gone platinum within forty-eight hours, had distinguished itself as the fastest-selling album in UK chart history to date. These achievements were certainly worthy of celebration. But beneath the heady euphoria there was a persistent undertow of unease for Bono, tinged with a degree of personal insecurity.

As the music world clamoured for Bono to be hoisted upon a pedestal as the latest icon, he stressed that he did not personally believe that he constituted what the archetypal idol ought to look, or feel, like. Physically, he believed that he most resembled a manual worker; his broad square hands, he said, looked more like those of a bricklayer.

This was a genuinely held belief and not false modesty, even though, in spring 1987, Bono probably looked his rock rebel best. Whether he let his thick dark brown hair hang loose about his shoulders or ruthlessly scraped it back off his face into a slick ponytail, he favoured the macho look, with dark waistcoats worn over sleeveless T-shirts, often with heavy chains or a large crucifix dangling round his neck.

Bono's unwillingness to grab this unconditional adoration with both hands reflected his search for a deeper meaning to what he stood for. As did his caution – if that was what it was – about buying into the massive media hype surrounding *The Joshua Tree*.

His caution seemed more understandable once it emerged that initially he had not had total confidence in the album's suitability for release right then. Bono has admitted that, at the eleventh hour, he had rung the band's manager, Paul McGuinness, expressing fears that the album would not sell into double figures.

Bono's opinion was by no means shared by the record-buying public around the world. The immediate reaction, both at street level and critically, was that, with this work, the four had hit a musical and lyrical peak. By virtue of its uniqueness, *The Joshua Tree* had firmly crowbarred U2 into the highest ranks of rock's hierarchy.

The album's unusual title is sometimes said to have been

inspired by the name of the Californian desert town in which the American singer/songwriter Gram Parsons (of The Flying Burrito Brothers) had been found dead in 1973. More straightforwardly, it is thought to have been called after the huge desert tree of that name, one example of which featured on the album cover.

On the album itself, weighty questions about spirituality, social responsibility and conscience, as well as morality, and attacks on terrorism, injustice and political oppression, were all raised within its tracks.

Some critics were prompted to quiz the band on whether they really thought such lyrics stood any chance of substantially altering or influencing situations for the better. Invariably, U2's answer was that they just hoped their songs might make people stop and consider exactly what was going on around them.

As ever, there was a thin dividing line between raising such topics as issues deserving of critical scrutiny, and being sanctimonious. Bono was alive to the risk of U2 being seen as a band that was attempting to solve all the world's ills. Whenever he detected the likelihood of this, he would hammer home the message that U2 were basically a noisy rock band to be enjoyed. Larry Mullen too stressed that those who came along to gigs simply to bang their heads against the wall in time to the music were equally welcome. This fail-safe mechanism always kicked in to prevent U2 from being perceived as rock missionaries.

Whilst *The Joshua Tree* was obviously a group effort, Bono's development as a songwriter had patently taken another huge leap forward. He imbued his lyrics on this album with a new vision and passion. And their effectiveness owed much to his ability to accurately take the pulse of the world around him.

In this respect, it patently helped that Bono had not bought into the usual drug-fuelled rock and roll lifestyle. His argument was that if a lyricist was so utterly removed from any real semblance of reality, was not grounded, not sentient to what truly mattered in people's everyday lives, then what, of any worth, could that person possibly write about?

Roughly a decade after U2 started out, Bono's approach to song-writing was still that ideas gestated best in his subconscious first. He then responded emotionally to those thoughts. He was still just as disorganized and would scribble lyrics on whatever came to hand, with the result that he was occasionally prone to misplacing his work.

But what also remained unchanged was his determination to lay on the line issues which, if addressed at all in music, usually tended to be presented in less direct fashion. In this respect certain tracks zoomed into sharp focus. For example, 'Mothers of the Disappeared' highlighted the sinister situation in El Salvador where young men were going missing without a trace. While 'Bullet the Blue Sky' – with its references to US foreign policy at that time – was unhesitatingly described by drummer Larry Mullen as a 'scathing attack on America'.

It frankly baffled Mullen that Americans – famed for their powerful sense of patriotism – could roll up in droves to enjoy a number that so blatantly exposed the band's contradictory feelings about their country.

US citizens, though, proved determinedly that, for their part, they felt no ambivalence towards the Irish rock band. For days before tickets were due to go on sale for the New York City and New Jersey gigs, hundreds formed queues, huddling in poor weather outside Manhattan-based ticket outlets to ensure they were not disappointed.

Without doubt, this world tour would be U2's most vital yet. Conscious of the building anticipation for the start of the US leg, they had responded to the pressure by over-rehearsing which soon made Bono's already gravelly voice slightly hoarse. And bassist Adam Clayton viewed the upcoming onslaught as frightening because of the heightened level of expectation.

All this made it doubly unwelcome when some American commentators, in feverish anticipation, began comparing U2 to the Beatles. Bono immediately tried to douse this one on the band's behalf by stating, 'We think we are overrated.'

Time magazine disagreed. In reviewing U2's series of tumultuous live performances as the tour travelled to thirteen cities, dropping anchor with five final shows in New Jersey in the second week of May, it unequivocally declared, 'U2 carries the day, but Bono carries the show.'

Throughout, the singer did indeed now prowl the stage with even more flair. And the tantalizingly smouldering sensuality with which he impregnated his lyrics was more potently alluring than obvious sexual posturing could ever have been.

The American tour would end on a happier and more relaxed note than it had begun. On their arrival in Tempe, Arizona, they discovered that the state's recently installed Republican governor, Evan Mecham, had cancelled the annual commemoration of the late Martin Luther King's birthday.

Affronted, the band briefly considered cancelling their three sold-out gigs there in protest. But instead, they decided to make a financial contribution to a committee already specifically set up to try to have this observance reinstated. At the same time, by releasing a statement, they made public their joint feelings of disgust over this official slight to King's memory.

And on their opening night at Arizona State University, from the stage, Bono delivered a thinly veiled swipe at Evan Mecham, whilst also obliquely urging the people of Arizona not to forget the late human rights leader. For good measure, the band drove home their own stance with a poignant, soaring rendition of their tribute number 'Pride (In the Name of Love)'.

Unknown to the 15,000-strong opening night crowd, U2 had endured their own mini-drama when their final rehearsal, the day before, had come to an abrupt and bloody stop. Things had appeared to be going smoothly until Bono, whilst singing, lost his footing as he stepped up on to a raised section of the stage. Off-balance, he fell heavily. His face landed on a footlight, thereby splitting open his chin. With blood soaking through a hastily provided towel, and dazed and ashen-faced, the injured singer was taken by ambulance to a nearby hospital where his wound had to be stitched.

On opening night itself his stitches were masked by stage make-up. But by so far into the show nothing could conceal the fact that Bono was having trouble with his voice. As he mowed his way through a mix of old favourites and the new material, he made intense efforts to overcome his difficulty in hitting and sustaining certain notes, a by-product of which was that these numbers assumed an added angry edge.

Initially it energized the audience but his band mates quickly realized that Bono was struggling. Finally, placing his fingers around his pain-filled throat, Bono gave up and stopped singing. With scarcely a pause, the crowd stepped into the breach and, en masse, sang the missing words back to the band. It was a special show of understanding unity, particularly when, as Bono then ploughed on, for the remainder of the gig the audience promptly participated whenever necessary.

Edge later talked of U2's amazement at the spectacle that the fee-paying crowd – not the band – had provided that night, admitting that but for their generosity of spirit the band would have been in serious trouble.

It was a moving and unusual way to start a tour, particularly one on which so much was riding. But it was also a shaky start that was compounded when, next day, due to Bono's inability to sing, for the first time in the band's history they had to call off a show so that he could receive medical attention.

The gig, though, would be quickly rescheduled. And fears that more postponements might be on the cards were allayed when doctors diagnosed nothing more serious than laryngitis. This cleared up sufficiently quickly to allow Bono and company to be back on the stump within a couple of days. Progress after that was good, with confirmed superstar status awaiting them by the time the final note rang out in New Jersey.

Less than ten days later the band would embark on an assault on Europe – not really enough time to rest up, physically or emotionally. This was particularly true for Bono who had already experienced strain on the homefront in the first quarter of the year.

Earlier in spring, he had been openly admitting that some aspects of his personal life were 'a mess'. The home he now shared with Ali was a fortified, three-storey, formidable-looking, granite watch tower, access to each level being by a single spiral staircase.

But between their individual commitments – Bono's to the band and Ali's to her studies at Dublin's University College where she was now a political science student – they did not have enough chances to spend time together at this remarkable home. And all this came on top of 1986 having already been a tough year on them. The strain now showed in each of the two occasionally operating on a short fuse.

Admiringly, Bono often reveals that his wife is not the kind of woman to allow herself to become a decorative ornament to be dusted off and paraded on her famous husband's arm and that, on the contrary, she is immensely independent. Still, he managed to misread her likely reaction when, following a transatlantic telephone call that he had made to her whilst in Arizona, Bono was concerned enough at what he thought were signs of low spirits in Ali, to ask her family to look out for her during his absence.

One pithy phone call later from his wife, left Bono in no doubt that she had not appreciated that particular consideration. Although Ali, in her anger, had hung up on him, she flew out unannounced soon afterwards to join her husband in America. And they had enjoyed her five-day stay before having to part again.

Although it came with the territory, it was hard for Bono to be separated so often from Ali. But he did find that there was some consolation in the fact that he was not a solo performer. Bono valued the companionship of being part of a band with three long-standing friends, any one of whom he could go and shake awake in the small hours to talk over any problems with.

Their friendship was also strengthened by the fact that they all continued to live in fairly close proximity to one another around Dublin. During the brief breaks between touring in spring and summer 1987, Bono often took himself round to Larry Mullen's house, also situated in Howth, to spend time with probably the quietest member of the group.

Aside from the music they had other things in common. Larry too was married to his school sweetheart and, although he lived in comfort, there was nothing materialistic or flashy about him. Like Bono, Mullen considered it crass to flaunt vulgar and insensitive displays of wealth in a country where so many people were trapped on the dole queue.

Soon back on the road, U2's European experiences resumed in explosive style in Rome in late May 1987. The mounting hysteria surrounding their appearances now led the band members to have to run for it if they were discovered in any public place. And in the Italian capital the sheer number of fans mobbing their hotel necessitated an armed escort to and from the stadium gig – a precaution that amused and appalled the band in equal measure.

In mid-June they played two consecutive nights at London's Wembley Stadium, with a similar double-header at Dublin's Croke Park a fortnight later. Interspersed with these gigs, the band also materialized in Switzerland, Germany, France, Holland, Spain and elsewhere, throughout the sunshine months.

Also brightening up their firmament, in addition to a nightly dose of live adulation, was more recording glory. On 13 June 'I Still Haven't Found What I'm Looking For' with the B side 'Spanish Eyes'/'Deep In the Heart' hit number six in the British charts. But the melodic single, aided by an infectiously appealing laid-back video which they had filmed weeks before on the streets of Las

Vegas, proved that in America U2 were still on a roll. It became their second consecutive US number one hit in the space of four months.

By the time the European leg of the world tour ended in early August, and before the band made a triumphant return to the States a month later, U2 had truly come to represent the beacon of youthful idealism. This was a role from which all four had often wished to distance themselves. But the summer had undeniably been a time for rallying calls and speechmaking on Bono's part.

Already U2's official fan magazine, *Propaganda*, had been known to carry notices encouraging people to write letters to various world governments and regimes urging the release of that particular country's prisoners of conscience. But it was not only on behalf of Amnesty International that Bono had taken to speaking up. He had also raised issues including Third World poverty, specific cases and kinds of injustice, and the global squandering of billions on developing weapons of mass destruction while curable killer diseases still ravaged great swathes of the earth for want of a fraction of this money being spent on food and medicine.

On 11 June 1987, too, the British Conservative government had won a third term in office. Initially, this time round, Bono had intended to keep his powder dry on this political issue, particularly since by now he could not see either of the two main opposition political parties, Labour or the Liberals, as representing serious alternative solutions. But he felt strongly about the massive unemployment. 'Words are failing me at the moment,' he declared, as he predicted the start of a new and frightening political era.

His deep-seated frustration over some of these causes triggered a matching sense of outrage in his enthralled audiences. It did not seem to matter to Bono if he had originally decided to refrain from indulging in this kind of incendiary audience address. Once the adrenalin was pumping, he inevitably got swept up in the heat of the moment. Some critics began to balk at this practice. And by July a number of journalists took to describing some U2 gigs as 'angst-ridden shows' but in a strangely fan-friendly fashion.

U2's style had always been different live. In the studio they enjoyed experimenting. But stage work was all about raw power, the whole essence of theatre, and creating a closeness with an audience. When sections of some crowds took to slavishly copying Bono's every gesture, though, questions were inevitably asked as to the desirability of evoking what could be construed as mindless devotion.

Bono, however, always categorically refuted any suggestion that U2's followers were anything other than independent free thinkers. Indeed, manipulation and the blurring of lines between reality and fiction was one of Bono's pet targets – he would often warn of the dangers of allowing the media to manufacture a nation of unquestioning sleepwalkers.

Closer to home, Bono was faced with another dilemma by summer 1987. He *did* enjoy, he insisted, the fact that U2 were being hailed as the biggest band in the world. And he *did* appreciate the luxuries that such fame brought, like having a private jet put at their disposal. But he still gave out contradictory signals.

With his Irish charm, optimism and wit, Bono had lost none of his beguiling attraction but at the same time he held on to his tendency towards making near pessimistic pronouncements. When this came at a time when most other rock stars in such a fêted position would have revelled in their success, it took on an extra significance. Conscious of the irony of having attained the fame which they had set out to achieve, only to crave the anonymity that was once theirs, he talked of the 'glass cage of success'.

He also became more anxious about U2's ability to live up to the accolades being heaped upon them and, moreover, being able to do so in a meaningful sense. Bono would confound an interviewer who was busily trying to trumpet the band's achievements by lamenting what he called the many opportunities already lost along the way.

He was patently wary, too, of predicting any longevity in the business for U2. When weighing up the pros and cons of their new situation, Bono even blamed his increased wealth for isolating him from some of those people with whom he had once been friendly. All in all, it is not hard to see why the band began to acquire a less-than-flattering reputation as killjoys, who were unable to enjoy their own good fortune. Bono acknowledged the existence of their some-what po-faced image, but he insisted that, although they took their music and their beliefs very seriously, they did not take *themselves* too seriously.

In parallel to the band's image, Bono was fast becoming known as a quasi-political, quasi-religious figure in rock. It was understood by now that he was attracted to the radical side of Christianity. The Son of God, Bono had often pointed out, was the one who, according to the Bible, had entered the temple and had angrily chucked the greedy money-lenders out on to the street. Bono deliberately referred to religion and Christianity as two separate entities. And he emphatically believed that a crucial cornerstone of Christianity had to be a strong commitment to social justice.

By now he was, however, toying with busting loose from the role of responsible rock star. At least, there was a two-way struggle going on in his head. On the one hand, he knew which principles he wanted to live by. Yet, at the same time, he was acknowledging that part of him could be temporarily attracted to the freer attitudes to material things that had been adopted by the rock stars of yesteryear.

With characteristically startling candour, he owned up – in the midst of the swirl of media attention generated by *The Joshua Tree*'s success – to believing that he was at risk of losing control of his life as a rock star.

He likened this rollercoaster life to riding the crest of a wave – in other words, living with the ever-present, knife-edge reality of there being one crucial moment when falling off means sinking beneath the waves. 'I want to say, "We're not in danger",' he said. 'But, actually, I do think we are.'

Already concerned about the levels of radiation contaminating the Irish Sea, in June 1992 U2 agreed to join environmental groups protesting against plans to develop a Thermal Oxide Reprocessing Plant at Sellafield in Cumbria, England.

Clowning with US soldiers on peace-keeping duty in Sarajevo. But the human face of the conflict was borne strongly upon Bono when some local children surreally presented him with two gift-wrapped spent bullets which had been dug out of their family bedroom wall.

This danger, real or imaginary would pass, by which time Bono would ultimately emerge as having come to the conclusion that it was possible to choose which traditions of rock behaviour to embrace and which to reject.

Among the traditions that he would not accept was the opportunity that fame afforded to show arrogant disregard for others, particularly people in a band's employ or susceptible fans. Bono stated that there was indubitably an inflated power in being a celebrity and that to suggest otherwise took either a degree of duplicity or monumental fake humility.

Stardom, which nevertheless he would never deny could be exciting and stimulating, also embraced other less welcome aspects. These included, for instance, the threat presented by the more calculating female who viewed one clandestine night of passion with U2's frontman as potentially lucrative tabloid fodder. Or the crazed nutter out to claim notoriety by extinguishing the singer's life, and who could be any one of the apparently innocent ordinary faces in the crowd.

Bono avoided the chance of obliging the former, but the latter became a real and present possibility. Soberingly, he revealed that he knew of people who had already claimed that they wanted to kill him. Sadly, death threats are almost an occupational hazard for celebrities, but that would have been scant comfort when nearing the seventh anniversary of John Lennon's murder.

None of this stopped Bono, however, from continuing to meet fans at close quarters in unplanned and, therefore potentially, dangerous circumstances. U2's itinerary hardly allowed for it, but he did manage a short break again during the long European phase and briefly returned to his home outside Dublin.

Just as he maintained his accessibility to the media, so those fans who were resourceful enough to find out where his home was located and who felt sufficiently intrepid to bang on his front door, were not turned away. Taken off guard, Bono inevitably ended up asking the uninvited visitors inside for a cup of tea.

Inwardly he would later castigate himself for having been too soft and indeed he once cited his own reasonableness as being what he disliked most about himself. For the rest of the time, any nights off between gigs had been spent with the band recording B-sides of singles – studio sessions that usually stretched into the small hours.

The elevation brought by *The Joshua Tree* did not set any musical parameters in Bono's mind. Like the others in the band he saw it not so much as a pinnacle achievement but as the dawn of a new era. And music wasn't the only call on his attention.

Despite being in the brightest spotlight of his career, Bono sometimes pondered a creative life away from the rock scene. His youthful attraction to acting still lingered and he had already been offered a handful of minor parts. He also dabbled with painting, but the art of capturing the true essence of the living moment through a camera lens grabbed him more. He had even had displayed, in a Dublin gallery, a selection of his photographs taken in the latter days of his Ethiopian trip.

Bono also has strong urges to be an author. Having co-scripted a play with his friend Gavin Friday, he has a growing collection of writings which he may one day publish.

In September 1987 it was his day job, though, that pressed most on his mind and time. The last leg of U2's world tour would take the band back to North America for a string of fifty dates.

They were returning in good form. The day after the tour kicked off in Uniondale, New York, 'With Or Without You' won the Viewers' Choice trophy at the fourth annual MTV Video Music Awards.

The following day, on 12 September, U2's latest single 'Where the Streets Have No Name'/'Silver and Gold'/'Sweetest Thing' entered the UK charts at number four. Although it would stall in the American charts four weeks later at number thirteen, the accompanying video had created quite a stir.

Filmed back in late March, U2 had emulated the Beatles' famous January 1969 stunt (when the Fab Four had appeared unexpectedly on the roof of the Apple building in London's Savile Row). The band had performed instead on the roof of a rundown building in downtown Los Angeles.

As had happened in London nearly two decades earlier, the noise brought people pouring out of shops and offices into the paved areas below, craning their necks and shielding their eyes with their hands to glimpse the four figures so far above them.

Thousands are said to have gathered and the scenes certainly looked chaotic when overhead cameras picked out a growing number of agitated, helmeted Los Angeles cops who milled about, trying to shepherd the enthusiastic crowd and to maintain order. Meanwhile, Larry Mullen, Adam Clayton and Edge roared into the number 'Where the Streets Have No Name' with Bono in full flight, his flowing locks flying and his loose shirt billowing in the breeze as he sang. The band performed until the police arrived on the rooftop and shut them down.

This apparently impromptu performance had, in fact, been carefully telegraphed in advance to ensure a crowd and media attention. Not coy about the ploy, Bono later came clean that they had leaked news of their intention but that he still found the actual experience terrifying. Nonetheless it made for an exhilarating video.

The more controlled environment of touring meanwhile continued, taking U2 from state to state on now familiar territory, in the knowledge that each night was ripe with possibilities.

What no one could plan for were real-life events that could metaphorically throw a hand grenade into proceedings. One such event occurred in early November. Just before the band were due to walk on stage in Denver, Colorado, they heard news of an IRA bombing that outraged the world. An explosive device had been detonated during a Remembrance Day service at Enniskillen in Northern Ireland, killing thirteen people.

All such atrocities are appalling, but to blow up people who were gathered to remember and honour their war dead was particularly despicable. And the band took the news very badly.

Bono admits that he is interested in the anatomy of terrorism. That is to say, he is interested in trying to understand the dark and complex motives that drive those who are willing to perpetrate aspects of what he calls the modern-day holocaust. In a few years' time he and U2 would do what they could to encourage support for a momentous peace agreement in Northern Ireland. Right then, all he could feel was a mixture of intense rage, revulsion and pain on behalf of the victims and their families.

Being Bono, he was not slow to lash out verbally at those individuals in America who love to romanticize the 'Struggles', and at those who funded terrorist organizations from a safe, comfortable distance. Anyone unwise enough to attempt to talk to the singer in sentimental tones about the Troubles in the 'old country, back home' received extremely short shrift. His concentration, however, had to revert to the task at hand as, after that night's gig, the tour trundled on, with one brief incursion into Canada.

One of the tour's most curious moments came on 18 November when, at the Los Angeles Coliseum, U2 opened for itself, playing the support set as the Dalton Brothers, a fictitious country/rock outfit. Taking the play-acting to its limit, each member even assumed a pseudonym. Edge became Luke, Mullen was Duke, while Clayton curiously opted for Betty. Bono meanwhile became Alton Dalton which, though it was short-lived, must go down as one of his earliest alter-egos.

Having spent nearly two-thirds of 1987 on the road, the tour wrapped just before Christmas. Before the year's end another single, 'In God's Country'/'Bullet the Blue Sky', was released in America. Copies imported into Britain managed to help it to chart, but only at number forty-eight (four places lower than its American best).

But this could not take the dazzling shine off what had been an extraordinary year. The last twelve months had seen U2 indisputably established as the biggest rock band in the world. And their figurehead, Bono, was now a fully paid-up member of the topmost ranks of revered rock frontmen.

CHAPTER 8

Saviour

U2'S DEIFICATION CONTINUED in the New Year. First, the band lifted the prize for Best International Group at the annual Brit Awards held in London. Then, on 2 March 1988, at the 30th Grammy Awards held at Radio City Music Hall in New York, they collected two of the most prestigious trophies of the night – Album of the Year, for *The Joshua Tree*, and Best Rock Performance By a Duo or Group for their hit, 'I Still Haven't Found What I'm Looking For'.

Edge and Bono shared the acceptance speech honours, with the singer raising ripples of laughter from the live audience at his tongue-in-cheek, self-deprecating cracks about how hard it was to shoulder all the world's woes.

However, Bono also knew that at that moment he had a television audience of approximately 50 million watching him. What he was really itching to be serious about was the dark issue of apartheid and the current plight of many oppressed people in South Africa.

Touching on the anti-apartheid struggle, he managed to mention Archbishop Desmond Tutu and the leading churchman's tireless work in the battle. But when his words received a polite, but distinctly tepid, response he pulled back, and confined the rest of his comments to music.

Backstage, the press pack was less restrained. With questions being fired at the band from all angles, a disembodied voice from the assembled crowd of reporters then asked the four what it felt like to be described as 'the band that has saved the world'.

To a man, U2 preferred to discourage such runaway exaggeration but, as they had fast discovered, it was a difficult juggernaut to disable. Already Larry Mullen had categorically stated that they had absolutely no interest in being seen as spokesmen for a generation. Also in recent months, both the drummer and Adam Clayton had started to kick against the obsession among some sections of the music media with intellectualizing U2's music. Bono's halo as resident rock saviour, though, would soon begin to slip.

After that night, U2 remained in America. For the first time in several years they would not be touring. Instead, from April onwards, Bono and the others focused their energies on working in Los Angeles on another album. And it wasn't just an album. They had a new and ambitious project in mind, the groundwork for one aspect of which had first been laid in 1987 when director Philip Joanou had filmed U2 during the Joshua Tree Tour. The director wanted to make a live documentary movie about the band's American tour. And this big-screen rockumentary was to be accompanied by a double album soundtrack.

Produced by Jimmy Iovine and called *Rattle and Hum*, the double album was a collage of new studio recorded tracks, a selection of cover versions, and live – usually lengthy – numbers from gigs going back over the last two years.

U2's main intention with this project had been to illustrate visually and musically the positive influence that American music stars had had on them. And so the legendary blues giant B. B. King had guested on the gutsy rhythm and blues number 'When Love Comes to Town'. The four collaborated on songs with Bob Dylan and they had also recorded at the famous Sun Studios in Memphis,

Tennessee, long since immortalized as the recording birthplace of Elvis Presley, with whom Bono had become fascinated.

The Sun Studios five-hour session made a lasting impression on Bono; the ambience of the ultra basic recording facilities, which are deliberately frozen in time, throwing up the sense (and, even fancifully, the scent) of another era.

Bono was excited to be singing into the self-same microphone as Presley had used and he later ruefully confessed that he only wished he had had Presley's voice to go with it. Taking their acute awareness of working in the American legend's original stomping ground to extremes, Edge even jokingly remarked that he was honoured to use the same toilet facilities as the King.

Then it was back to the present – and post-production for both U2's new album and the documentary movie took place amid the hi-tech sophistication of the A & M Studios in Los Angeles as autumn began to beckon.

Thus far, things had been moving at a less hectic pace than in previous years, although it would begin to quicken soon enough. Before it did, in September, Bono and Edge took time out for a very special involvement with the singer Roy Orbison for whose comeback album they had co-written a song called 'She's a Mystery to Me'.

To Bono, this involvement had an extraordinary, almost weird, back story that had begun roughly a year before. He revealed that while on the Joshua Tree Tour he had been toying on and off with the rudiments of a new song, one which was possibly to be recorded by another artiste.

The song was at last beginning to take shape in his head one night backstage and he had literally just wondered aloud to the others which recording star, vocally, it might be best suited to. At that very moment a knock on the band's dressing room door brought a security guard with the news that Roy Orbison and his wife Barbara, who had attended the gig, were outside in the corridor asking if they could meet U2.

Soon after admittance, the unassuming singer – also famous for perpetually wearing dark glasses, as well as for his high-register vocal style and his 1964 number one hit 'Oh Pretty Woman' – asked Bono, 'You wouldn't happen to have a song for me, would you?' Whereat the rest of U2 stared, dumbstruck, at their apparently omniscient frontman. He was himself temporarily lost for words, struck by the amazing coincidence.

Quickly retrieving his scattered wits, Bono ran through 'She's a Mystery to Me' for their backstage visitor, who instantly adored it. For Roy Orbison then, Bono and Edge had set about crafting the strangely haunting number. And twelve months or so later, in September 1988, Bono stood beside Orbison in the studio as the American recorded the song.

Bono found the whole experience startling. He later recalled, of watching Orbison at work, 'He hardly opened his mouth and I wondered if he was taking the mick.' During the playback afterwards, however, Bono was blown away by the timeless quality that Orbison had seemingly effortlessly embroidered into the song.

He describes the older singer as having the voice of an angel, explaining that there are rare, crystallizing moments when something very special can happen to a vocalist in the recording studio. He said, 'As a singer there's just that moment when your voice is above you.' And that day Roy Orbison 'had it in abundance'.

'She's a Mystery to Me' would appear on Roy Orbison's album *Mystery Girl* which, released the following year in February 1989, hit numbers two and five respectively in Britain and America. Sadly, Orbison did not live to savour his success. Just months after that recording session with U2, in early December 1988, the 52-year-old singer died of a heart attack.

But, fresh from the studio session with Roy Orbison, Bono's pride at his involvement with someone whom he considers to be one of the greats was clear. At the same time, further confirmation of U2's own popularity came with the news, published in the September 1988 issue of the respected American financial publication

Forbes, that the band, having earned an estimated US$42 million during 1987 and 1988, now ranked eleventh in the list of the world's forty top-earning entertainers.

Also at this time – a full ten years after landing their first record-ing contract – the band finally secured their first number one in the British singles' chart, with the release on 1 October of the velvety rockabilly number 'Desire', backed by 'Hallelujah (Here She Comes)'.

This was followed, three weeks later, by the double album *Rattle and Hum* which reigned supreme both in Britain and in America where it was launched in mid-November. And in between, on 27 October 1988, the world premiere of the film *Rattle and Hum* took place in Dublin.

That they had scored another commercial hit with this latest album was accepted. But the project in the round was, critically speaking, a different matter. Many critics, fairly or otherwise, looked upon their release of the film together with the soundtrack album as an exercise in self-indulgent, pretentious vanity.

With *Rattle and Hum*, they had certainly broken away from being labelled as an issues-oriented band. But now some reviewers took exception to what they regarded as U2's newfound absorption with American musical roots, even though again the fans obviously did not feel unduly put out. As was proved when the last single of the year, 'Angel of Harlem'/'No Room at the Heartbreak Hotel' – the A side being a lilting, nostalgic tribute to the jazz singer Billie Holiday – nestled at number nine in Britain in time for Christmas.

As for the *Rattle and Hum* rockumentary itself, with its onstage footage, Bono's propensity to make speeches now grated with some. One critic also wondered, when the singer railed against the IRA, the continuing abomination of apartheid or any other important issue, why he did so in a droning accent that sounded suspiciously like that of the late American Western actor John Wayne.

Another commentator would later state that when U2 undertook this film of themselves, 'the potential dangers of Spinal Tap style hubris were obvious'. Such a prospect must have appalled the band. The last thing they wanted was to have the least whiff of ridicule or arrogance attached to them.

At the turn of the year this air of misfire coincided with the band's plan to withdraw from the spotlight for a while anyway. There were no grounds for any loss of confidence. Their last two singles, 'Desire' and 'Angel of Harlem', had hit numbers three and fourteen respectively in America. And in February 1989 the annual music award season yielded the band another crop of honours.

At London's Royal Albert Hall, U2 were yet again voted Best International Group at the Brit Awards. Then, just over a week later, for the second consecutive year, the four picked off the Grammy Award for Best Rock Performance by a Duo or Group, this time for the single 'Desire'. And another Grammy came their way for Best Performance Music Video for the energetic 'Where the Streets Have No Name'. Meanwhile, the new single 'When Love Comes To Town', on which B. B. King had guested, peaked at number six in mid-April.

Lying fallow for a while was not a bad idea, however. Bono welcomed periods that allowed time for re-evaluation, scarce though they might be. And lately he had been in a reflective mood anyway.

The reviewers who had criticized U2's apparently sudden interest in American gospel, blues and jazz had failed to take into account that, along with the others, prior to embarking on the *Rattle and Hum* project, Bono had realized that there was a journey of discovery to be undertaken.

By his own admission, for a long time Bono had felt no sense of belonging musically to any established tradition. He drew parallels between Irishmen and black people, both often feeling rudderless and like outsiders. But, rather than this being a negative thing, the search for an identity, he maintained, was what being an artiste was truly all about. And, for him, a good deal of that search had been satisfied through discovering a strong affinity between American and Irish traditional musical roots.

But it went even deeper than that. Bono is proud of being Irish. During the band's earliest forays into America he had frequently made it clear that U2 were Irish and therefore separate from the then influx of British pop stars who were penetrating the US music scene. But being an Irishman also allowed him to feel a kinship with the black man because, as he stated, although both races possessed soul and spirit, they had both, at one time, been the underdogs.

Bono maintained that, long before the politically correct world of today, the Irish had been described as 'white niggers'. And he declared, 'I take that as a compliment', explaining that, musically, many of his most profound inspirations had been drawn from coloured people.

Beyond music, on a socio-political level his thoughts never strayed far from Martin Luther King and King's message of non-violent resistance. When Bono contrasted this ethos with the continuing terrorist activities ravaging Ireland he felt deeply the essential need for those involved to somehow move away from confrontation. Writing in the Irish press at the end of 1988, Bono declared, 'If war in Northern Ireland is what it means to be Irish, then we must redefine Irishness.'

And musically it was not only the past and the present that preoccupied Bono. As the decade entered its final months, the future of popular music concerned him. Bono disdained the machine-produced noises that had been passing for music for some time now, and which had systematically dehumanized the art. He predicted – wrongly, as it turned out – that the next decade would steer away from such soulless synthetic sounds.

But whatever his professional and political passions, his personal feelings took precedence when, on 10 May 1989, Bono's twenty-ninth birthday, Ali presented her husband with their first child, a girl whom they called Jordan.

Delighted with his daughter, Bono now viewed fatherhood differently. Even two years ago, he would have found the prospect quite daunting. Then, he had owned up to a lingering irresponsibility in his nature that he recognized might have handicapped his ability to cope, although he was always adamant that Ali was destined to be a terrific mother. Now it was a *fait accompli*, and he intended to ensure that he would not become the kind of dad whom the child eventually ends up having to take in hand.

Also in May 1989, Bono took time out to branch briefly into the world of literature. He acquitted himself well enough before an intrigued and appreciative audience at Dublin's Abbey Theatre when he made a guest appearance to give a very personal rendition of two poems by W. B. Yeats, which he had set to his own music.

Bono saw a correlation between songwriting and poetry. Only recently he had revealed that producer Brian Eno's personal view was that he (Bono) was even better at being a poet than he was at being a lyricist. The compliment, Bono believed, was rooted in the fact that the texture and rhythm of words held a strong sway with him when it came to articulating his emotions in song.

With his literary cap on, Bono now stated that a heightened sensitivity to words and their different nuances was inherently a very Irish trait. But, far from feeling that he had everything figured out, Bono was happy to remain open and receptive. And with his antenna eternally scoping for new musical inspiration, by summer 1989 he was becoming more appreciative of traditional Irish folk music.

The breather of the last few months could not go on indefinitely, however, and a return to work was now imminent. Six weeks after Jordan's arrival, U2's latest single was released, an emotive ballad appropriately titled 'All I Want is You'/'Unchained Melody'. It climbed to number four in Britain, which considerably bettered its performance in the States, where it ran aground at number eighty-three. And on the same day, 24 June, U2 also launched a twenty-three date tour of Australia – their second trip Down Under, which opened in Perth.

Throughout their antipodean antics, U2 basked in the usual attention. But soon after returning home to Dublin, the shine was briefly knocked off. On 6 August 1989 Adam Clayton had the dubious distinction of notching up the one-and-only drug-related incident attributed to any U2 member, when he was arrested in the car park of the city's Blue Light Inn for possession of marijuana.

Although Adam Clayton had always pursued a more rock and roll lifestyle he had never before been in this kind of trouble and it must have been a worrying and tense time. A drug conviction, too, can mean being forbidden to enter certain countries. And, in the case of a rock star, this can lead to problems when it comes to touring.

As it turned out, less than a month later, on 1 September, the situation was resolved. In place of a conviction for possession of marijuana it was agreed that Adam Clayton would donate money to the Womens' Aid and Refuge Centre in Dublin; the sum was reported to be somewhere in the region of £25,000.

With this matter closed, a return trip to Australia and New Zealand was on the cards later in the year. But before this, their eyes were turned on America. On 6 September U2 added to its bristling trophy chest by winning the prize for Best Video for the number 'When Love Comes to Town' at the MTV Music Awards ceremony in California.

Then, four days later, the giant NBC TV network broadcast a show called the 'International Very Special Arts Festival' at which U2 was one of the guests. This show, which would become an annual event, sought to celebrate achievements by physically and mentally handicapped artistes. With fellow guest performers including Hollywood star Michael Douglas, actress Lauren Bacall, ballet dancer Mikhail Baryshnikov and country singer Kenny Rogers, it was broadcast from the grounds of the White House in Washington DC.

At that time, the incumbent of the world's most famous address was President George Bush Senior, some of whose Republican politics Bono disagreed with. In the 1990s, under a new Democrat regime, Bono would become a not unfamiliar face in the corridors of power at 1600 Pennsylvania Avenue.

Within days of this broadcast Bono was back on the road with U2, as touring commitments were scheduled to occupy them to beyond the end of the year. Australia and New Zealand became the launchpad from where, after a brief break, they hit Japan in late November, before arriving in France mid-December for the start of their European tour dates.

Nearing the end of these commitments, U2 returned to Dublin to perform four gigs in the last week of December 1989 at The Point, formerly an old rail terminal and today one of Ireland's top live music venues.

Adding to the chill of winter, by now there was another sea change going on. Throughout the year the tide had been turning and now in the decade's dying days Bono's image as a rock saviour was under attack. His passion for speaking out about serious issues was meeting with threadbare tolerance in a press that was now more likely to see it as onstage sermonizing.

The danger with being set up as a Messianic figure is that one can easily become a figure of fun instead, and Bono began to find himself sent up in the newspapers. It was an uncomfortable position for the frontman. Edge remarked that one of his main fears was that this treatment might have the effect of stunting Bono's growth as a songwriter.

It was also a concern, shared by all four members of the band, that at the same time a disproportionate importance was constantly being placed now on whatever utterance they individually made. Edge deemed it to be potentially dangerous artistically, too, that the name U2 had become as well known as some brandname consumer products.

Bono acknowledged the downside to the massive media coverage the band had received in recent times. To promote the *Rattle and Hum* rockumentary, for example, gigantic posters of each individual band member had been plastered all over the place, to the point that Bono once frankly confessed, 'Even I would probably have hated us then!'

In a few years' time, the reaction to the whole *Rattle and Hum* project would level out. Eventually it would be seen, generally, as an idea of some merit but one that had spiralled out of control. But in 1989 the backlash that had begun over the *Rattle and Hum* album and rockumentary ended with Bono standing accused by journalists of exhibiting signs of excessive self-importance.

It culminated onstage at The Point. Sounding worryingly weary, Bono began to make fans uneasy when, during a short speech, after referring to the pleasure the band had derived from exploring once unfamiliar musical terrain, he began talking in terms of this being 'the end of something for U2'. He said these gigs were intended to be a party as much for the band as for the fans, and declared, 'We have to go away and dream it all up again.'

Bono called going away for a little while to think and perhaps try something different, 'no big deal'. But distraught fans, and a stunned music press drew a different conclusion. Rumours were quick to reverberate that, shockingly, the biggest band in the world was about to break up.

CHAPTER 9

Egotist

THE EXTENDED HIATUS lasted for almost two years, probably longer than anyone had anticipated, but Bono and U2 were not entirely forgotten. To begin with, the band's existing recent work attracted awards at the annual round-up in early 1990.

On 18 February they made off, for a satisfying third time, with the Best International Group prize at the Brit Awards held at the Dominion Theatre in London. In Bono's case, less than three weeks later he was also named in the United States by *Rolling Stone* readers, as Sexiest Male Rock Artist as well as Best Songwriter, the latter recognition being a source of particular pride to him.

Arriving at the milestone of his thirtieth birthday in May, Bono had everything a man might conceivably crave. He was in a stimulating and stable marriage, he had started a family, he was already financially secure for life, and he commanded the respect and adulation of millions of fans worldwide. Yet, to the eternally restless young man, it was still not enough to nourish his need for total fulfilment.

Neither was his musical compass to be set in the same direction anymore. The earnest tackling of world issues, until now done largely in an anthemic rock style, would give way to the agonies and ecstasies of sculpting a new U2 and the dismemberment of the righteous image of old.

It can have been no accident that, as the band were poised on the threshold of a new musical direction, they should opt to work in the one city in the world, right then, that was on the brink of a new beginning – Berlin.

In August 1961, after East Germany had suddenly sealed the border between East and West Berlin, a 6-foot high concrete wall had been erected frighteningly fast, topped with almost impenetrable rolls of barbed wire and guard towers. Over the years, the 28-mile long wall, with its armed checkpoints, was further fortified. This wall became a hated symbol of the Soviet Union's iron grip, and between 1961 and 1989 seventy-five people had been shot dead whilst trying desperately to escape over the wall.

Astoundingly dramatic changes were taking place in world politics during the death throes of the 1980s and these changes culminated on 9 November 1989 when the physical destruction of the Berlin Wall began. It started with mass demonstrations. Then, at midnight, thousands of people on both sides of the wall gave a collective almighty roar and started to pour through the checkpoints.

Jubilant, emotional and fiercely determined, people of all ages climbed up on top of the wall – some to dance in celebration of this momentous breakthrough, others to set about hacking with crude tools, or even their bare hands, at the loathed monument, dismantling it brick by brick. Eleven months after this physical breach of the wall, on 3 October 1990, came the official Liberation and Reunification Day, when Germany again became one nation.

U2 flew into Berlin on the eve of this historic day, keen to be a part of the celebrations. Forty-five years after the end of the Second World War, Germany would be free and united once more.

Virtually fresh off the plane, Bono, and the others, immediately took to the thronged streets, intending to join in the nearest parade.

Expecting joyous hysteria, it began to dawn on Bono that something was not quite right about the atmosphere around him. The penny eventually dropped that they had inadvertently joined the wrong party. It turned out that the people around him were those who remained hardline Communists and the march he had joined was one to protest for the wall to be rebuilt.

However, despite this initial hiccup, it was indeed a memorable night. The official rebirth of the nation was ushered in at midnight with a long rolling peal from the Freedom Bell at Schönberg City Hall. Thousands roared, cheered, cried and hugged total strangers amid a forest of wildly waving black, red and gold flags, while spectacular fireworks splintered the night sky above.

Even after the crowds eventually dispersed, for Bono the emotive aspect of the event was not yet over. Having arrived only hours earlier and plunged into the melée, the band had taken temporary accommodation for the night in a former guesthouse in the east side of the capital.

On rising at a still early hour the following morning and going downstairs, Bono was startled to see a collection of people gathered in the hallway. Sleepy and unthinking, the singer asked them what they wanted in his house. To which the German family replied that, on the contrary, it was *their* home, a home to which they had only now been able to return. It was a strange and salutary moment that would stay with Bono for a long time.

After the dust had settled, U2 were left in Berlin facing the task for which, professionally, they had gone there – to seek the stimulus of recording in a new environment. That environment would become Hansa Studios although in the new year the recording sessions moved from Berlin to Dublin. But finding an inspirational locale was not the difficulty.

Bono believes U2 to be not so much a certain style and sound as essentially a spirit. This thinking, shared by the others, allowed the band in principle to strip away the layers down to base level, from which to begin forging a new sound. But in practice the search for a new identity was a struggle.

One of the band's producers, Brian Eno, confirmed that U2 entered into the work ready to rebel against their own mythology. Wearing the crown of champion means having to constantly push the boundaries, in order to stay ahead of the game. But experimentation also carries the risk of alienating fans.

As usual, the initial recording sessions produced a large pool of skeletal songs that all showed potential. The long, ruthless process of elimination necessary to select the tracks that were worthy of being intensely reworked was made tougher still by the fact that Bono fought tenaciously on behalf of practically every idea that was threatened with rejection. These passionate appeals led Eno to teasingly christen the frontman the 'Mother Teresa of Abandoned Songs'.

Brian Eno was not a resident producer on this album, in the strict sense of being permanently at the helm in the studio throughout months of daily endeavour. That diligent post was filled by his collaborator Daniel Lanois, who was aided in his work by a recording engineer known simply as Flood.

Eno's involvement instead was to plug into proceedings at regular intervals for a series of week-long stretches. That way, he could bring a fresh pair of ears to bear on the material being recorded and make suggestions accordingly.

This also meant that he might occasionally unwittingly suggest abandoning some work over which, metaphorically, many tears and much sweat had been shed in his absence. But, far more often, the clear perspective he was able to bring to the project was valuable.

The making of a U2 album always requires a lot of stamina. No one denies that there were fraught moments during the many studio-bound months, and this creative tension placed a strain on the normally optimistic, good-humoured band members.

The endless discussions about the material also took up a lot of time. But, as the seasons inexorably changed outside, inside the studio U2 gradually began to chart their own new, hard-won musical landscape, with Bono chiselling out the lyrics that defined each song's individual persona.

Collectively, those songs emerged as the opposite of all that had gone before, and the new look U2 had a dark, raucous sexuality about it. The bleakness that had infiltrated some of the recording sessions was also traceable; while, as a lyricist, Bono revealed – more than ever before – an intriguing and intimate introspection.

According to Bono, rock music relies for its success upon a mix of mystique and mischief and he maintains that 'sex and music are the only mystical acts left'. This new music managed to fuse both the flesh and religious faith and also addressed the contradictory aspects of everyday life. In varying degrees, this provided the backbone of the new album.

The first new U2 single in twenty-eight months emerged on 2 November 1991. Called 'The Fly' and backed by 'Alex Descends Into Hell For a Bottle of Milk'/'Korova 1', it entered the UK charts at number one. It clearly showcased the favoured darker, experimental style and paved the way for the arrival at the end of the month of its parent album, *Achtung Baby*.

Forward-looking and innovative, this album was also wildly different from any of its predecessors. The post-punk influence at the band's outset, which had been superseded in the mid-1980s by American roots music, was now itself swamped by the sounds of electronic dance music. Bono saw it as a heavy album but one which, with its industrial, mechanical sound, only *pretended* to be trashy, disposable stuff.

Not everyone got the idea; 'The Fly' creaked to a halt in America at number sixty-one. But the band's courage in ditching their trademark trappings to exhibit an adventurous, groundbreaking spirit was sufficient to retain the loyalty of their core fans. While *Achtung Baby* lodged at number two in Britain, the album debuted at number one throughout the remainder of the record-buying world.

Reincarnated for the new decade, U2 were straining at the leash to be let loose live once more. And, before 1991 came to an end, plans were well advanced for the band to back their new, critically acclaimed album with a massive world tour that would prove to be an unforgettable extravaganza.

Back in January, the Gulf War had broken out in the Middle East, as the allied Nato countries combined to take on Saddam Hussein, whose Iraqi military forces had invaded neighbouring oil-rich Kuwait. Operation Desert Storm involved a systematic, sustained air-and-surface bombardment of Iraq. And for the first time a major conflict, fought with the latest high-tech weaponry, was brought to everyone in the western world, via the mass media. 'War in the comfort of your own home. Even better than the real thing,' said Bono caustically.

As a pacifist, Bono called the war madness. He was appalled at the callous tone of the news reports that daily covered successful allied strikes – strikes which, while executed clinically and after-wards explained efficiently, in reality still translated into piles of dead human beings.

Using the remote control on his television, Bono was chilled to find that he could switch from children's programmes to scenes of real-life man-made carnage, as deadly Cruise or Scud missiles were tracked live on screen homing in on their targets.

This devastating display drove home to him the awesome power of television. And it was part of the reason that U2 decided to make the enormous – not always positive – impact of telecommunications on people's lives the theme of their new tour, to be called Zoo TV.

Having slipped out another single, 'Mysterious Ways'/'('A' Solar Remix)', which peaked at number thirteen in the UK and number nine in the States in January 1992, the band began gearing up for the gruelling series of gigs due to begin the following month.

The branch of the band's organization which takes care of the massive merchandizing opportunities provided by touring also swung into action, preparing everything from U2 posters and Zoo

TV tour programmes, to band sweatshirts and T-shirts. This time, however, there was one item not usually listed among a rock band's memorabilia – condoms. *Achtung Baby* condoms were to be available for sale during the band's American tour: two for US$3.

This was not the first time the Irish supergroup had raised public eyebrows over condoms. Fourteen years ago, as unknowns battling to be heard in a disused Dublin car park, U2 had taken part in that gig in support of the movement which protested against Ireland's anti-contraception laws at the time.

Then, just under a year before, in February 1991, U2 had offered to pay a £500 (Irish) pounds fine on behalf of the Irish Family Planning Association (IFPA), when this association had been found guilty of selling condoms illegally at a Virgin Record store in the centre of Dublin.

The IFPA had issued a press release at the time, part of which had read:

> The band's management said tonight, 'U2 would like to pay the £500 fine imposed on the IFPA because the band feel the Irish Family Planning Association have much more important things to be doing than turning up in court. Furthermore, the group fully support the IFPA's call for the law on the sale of condoms in Ireland to be changed.'

In early 1992, Bono managed to get away from it all for a while. He made the most of his free time to be with Ali and their family, which had been increased the previous July with the birth of a second daughter, whom they had named Memphis Eve. Then, on 29 February, the tour kicked off, with the North American leg commencing at the Civic Center Arena in Lakeland, Florida.

By the early 1990s spectacular stage sets were common at rock gigs. But the US$1 million Zoo TV stage set was an unusually elaborate multimedia mish-mash of sound and vision.

The stage was dominated by a multitude of television monitors mounted at the back. These projected a host of dislocated images – some relayed from stage cameras, some from a hand-held camcorder wielded by Bono (which he trained at arm's length on himself while he sang), and some from randomly selected satellite channels showing anything from snatches of foreign television news footage to live cricket match coverage.

At other times, single words, phrases or short sentences in different colours leapt out from these screens at the audience in jumbled flashes, in an overload of subliminal messaging. To this bewildering mix was added the overwhelming sight of big screen video walls and, bizarrely, four old East German Trabant cars were suspended overhead in such a way that their gleaming headlights added to the swirling blaze of stage lighting. Not surprisingly, the band on the stage below was completely dwarfed.

Brian Eno later revealed that he had originated this extraordinary idea for a stage set. He had wanted U2 to offer a more innovative use of video walls. (In the past these devices had simply been used to project the figures on stage on to celluloid for the benefit of the fans at the back of a venue.)

On top of these stunning visuals, came a shock for Bono fans: their idol now appeared before them in a brand new guise. Over the years Bono had sometimes changed style, from favouring wide-brimmed hats to sporting a harshly slicked-back ponytail hairstyle, but had largely stuck with his trademark dressed-down look.

Now his rich brown, once shoulder-length, hair had been cut above the collar, styled in a coif, and dyed coal black. This was also the trip when he appeared not only as U2 frontman but also introduced a cast of alter-egos, beginning with the Fly and the Mirrorball Man.

The Fly was a semi-spoof, semi-sinister, cool character for whom Bono encased himself in raunchy, skin-tight, black leather from head to toe and hid his blue-grey eyes behind a pair of unusual, wraparound, bug-eyed dark glasses. The character reeked of self-parody and one seasoned rock commentator described the incarnation as being a blend of 'Jim Morrison shamanism and Jerry Lee Lewis narcissism'. Most, however, struggled to grasp its true meaning.

The Mirrorball Man, a flash guy decked out with blindingly bad taste in a glitzy silver suit and a Stetson, represented an amalgamation of all things phoney and avaricious. As this character, Bono would hold up a full-length mirror in front of himself before reverentially kissing his own reflection.

In the early stages of this tour Bono had not completely defined this persona but the Mirrorball Man was intended as a cross between a televangelist and a travelling performer. For Bono, the Mirrorball Man was someone who peddled a totally money-oriented religion – a pretty accurate reflection of what he felt was happening with religion in the 1990s.

Posing as these, and other, alter-ego characters, Bono minced and mock-strutted about the stage. It was a pretence, a decadent, trashy send-up of rock stardom. But the irony escaped many people.

More than simply dressing up, though, Bono was putting on a mask from behind which it was easier to say and do certain things. At times, these different personas almost seemed to be in danger of taking over, especially when Bono began talking in interviews about his alter-ego characters as if they were real people.

Naturally this extraordinary and chaotic circus attracted massive interest as U2 took the sold-out show on the road around America. And, onstage, Bono brought the bite of unpredictability to proceedings by coming up with a few grandstanding gestures. One example was one night in March; from the stage in Detroit he telephoned a local pizza parlour and ordered up a thousand pizzas to go – the pizzas were intended for the audience.

Staff at the startled fast food company, having satisfied themselves that it was not a hoax call, manfully rose to the occasion. They managed to come up with a hundred pizzas within an hour and the delivery men who arrived with the king-size takeaway each earned themselves a US$50 tip.

The carefully crafted stage act had its set pieces, including the introduction of an exotic belly dancer. During the song 'Mysterious Ways', she would undulate her body to the music, always staying tantalizingly just out of Bono's reach, allowing her floaty veils merely to brush against his outstretched fingertips, leaving him eternally teased.

At a certain point in the night the band would quit the main stage for a smaller square platform intimately set up on the floor of the auditorium. Then, for a while, they could revert to being four musicians communicating on a one-to-one basis with their fans.

Bounding into the spotlight each night, Bono put everything he had into his adrenalin-driven performances. Throwing dramatic shapes, he would also bind both arms tightly across his chest as, with his eyes squeezed shut, he crooned or alternatively screeched into the microphone. By the end of the night his jet black hair would be plastered across his beaded brow in separate sweaty streaks.

At times he sang from a prone position on the floor of the stage. Other times he would sing whilst dragging the mike stand behind him as if it were a lead weight. Like a performer in an off-the-wall Christian Revival show, he would be loose-limbed, shaking his body spasmodically, whilst waving his arms and hands above his head, hallelujah-style.

Totally consumed, to the point of nightly rendering himself completely drained, Bono climbed right into the various characters he had created. Indeed he inhabited these roles so closely that it was not always easy afterwards to quickly divest himself of them.

Bono had also developed a distinct policy towards concerts. If, on the night, a concert could not, for one or other reason, be fantastic, he maintained that he would rather it be poor. The band aimed for the tops every night but Bono's worst nightmare, it seemed, would be for the show to attract the insult of being classed as having been average.

The continual cycle of psyching himself up for a performance, only to be left bled dry next day, took its toll. The relentless discipline too of performing, regardless of whatever else might be going on behind the scenes (in his life or with his health) was something he came to consider as a form of fraud.

He believed that the practice of projecting a normalcy about what he did for a living, when it was far from a regular existence, was completely crazy. Walking on stage he said was a step of faith. Most times he held it all together in his head. If he did not, he felt that he was living a lie.

As a performer who had always sought a symbiosis with the fans, he sometimes could not help feeling that in a way the fee-paying customer owned him; a feeling that made him uncomfortable. It galled him that, in the final analysis, an entertainer might be no more than a puppet who performed on cue.

Whilst they were on the road the only U2 single to be released was the ballad 'One'/'The Lady with the Spinning Head'. Scaling the top ten in Britain in mid-March and, two months later, in America was not unexpected. But it was a chart performance that barely hinted at the evocative number's long-term impact.

Eight years later, in a poll of the hundred most influential records of all time, compiled by *Rolling Stone* magazine in conjunction with the giant cable music channel MTV, U2's 'One' ranked at an impressive number eight.

The American/Canadian leg of the Zoo TV World Tour ended in late April 1992. This left Bono scarcely a fortnight in which to touch base with his family before the band prepared to take the now much-talked about spectacle into Europe for a six-week carnival beginning in France in early May. After having played London's Earl's Court, it would end in Britain in mid-June.

Along the way U2 had welcomed onstage fellow guest music stars, including performers as diverse as vocalist Axl Rose who had been with Guns 'n' Roses on their own European tour. And in

Stockholm, on 11 June, Abba stars Bjorn Ulvaeus and Benny Andersson joined U2 for a rendition of Abba's classic 1976 hit 'Dancing Queen'.

The Swedish supergroup had produced a string of colossal hits in the 1970s and early 1980s but critically they had never been fashionable. It took two decades for Abba to – belatedly – begin to publicly receive their just critical acclaim.

Reflecting on his own past view of the hitmaking pop group, Bono said, 'It was the era of punk rock and Abba were to be beheaded. And I probably would have held the axe.' Their sin, he felt, had been that in his opinion Abba had not made boys' music. That blinkered view, he now admitted, had blinded him to the fact that in reality Abba were one of the greatest pop groups ever.

The sheer uplifting joy in Abba's music appealed to the frontman who confessed, 'That's what makes them extraordinary.' With Benny at the keyboards and Bjorn on guitar that night in Stockholm, Bono and U2 performed their own individual rendition of 'Dancing Queen'. Bono showed his delight at the end by declaring that they (U2) were not worthy, before then bowing in intentionally exaggerated, but genuinely affectionate, reverence to their guest performers.

By June 1992, U2 were only four months into a tour that would ultimately last for nearly two years but already Bono was openly exhibiting a new way of thinking. He said he had spent much of the 1980s fighting shy of facing the reality that U2 was a commercially successful band that had been helped to stardom by robust marketing backing. Like the others, he had been scared to acknowledge this machinery, for fear that it would somehow diminish the importance of the music itself. He had viewed success as being a 'big bad wolf'.

Now those fears and facades were apparently gone and he was glad of it. He described the process of embracing the 'bullshit' synonymous with commercial success as giving it a big kiss and making up with it. When he commented, 'I must say, it is great fun being pretentious,' it was hard to tell whether or not his tongue was firmly lodged in his cheek.

Around the same time, some of U2's fans were finding it difficult to interpret the intended irony of the Zoo TV experience, to decipher its warning against the effects of the subliminal messaging that goes on in modern life via telecommunication. Bono's reaction to the problem was uncompromising. 'If they don't get it, I don't give a fuck,' he stated.

And with regard to the raft of fans that U2 had accumulated in recent years purely because of their standing as the latest in-band (as distinct from the longstanding 'real' U2 fans) and who were now perhaps beginning to fall away, the frontman succinctly waved them off with the words, 'We don't need them'. Such forthright honesty kept him the darling of the interviewer.

Yet the more familiar Bono was still there, beneath the leathers and behind the bug-eyed shades. This was the Bono who, as in the summer of 1992, remained committed to retaining his home base in Eire and still found himself deeply concerned about matters north of the border. He had been commenting on such issues since his early twenties. Now, not long past his thirty-second birthday he stressed the need to keep striving to make Ireland the place its people really wanted it to be.

Before anyone could point out that, with his privileged position, he could easily bail out instantly if this state failed to materialize, he acknowledged it himself. But he also declared that, more than ever, he wanted to have his home in Ireland. And now he truly had a vested interest in the country's future because, as the father of two daughters, he had to consider the kind of environment in which they were destined to grow up.

Fatherhood, he claimed, had sharply increased his understanding of anger and of the origins of the primeval instinct to protect one's children. He told the press that in his view there was probably no more dangerous a person than a father.

It may have been dense stuff to some people, but Bono

staunchly believed that there had to be a way forward in which all that angry energy could be channelled towards finding a lasting peace in Ireland.

To Bono-watchers, here was the familiar politically minded frontman, who yet had disguised himself in this new series of weird incarnations. All in all, it added up to yet another aspect of this ever-evolving individual to get used to.

CHAPTER 10

Activist

FURTHER PROOF THAT BONO'S new hedonistic stage persona had not, in reality, altered the activist in him one bit came at the conclusion of the UK leg of the Zoo TV Tour in mid-June 1992. At this point, U2 got involved with a benefit gig organized by the worldwide environmental pressure group Greenpeace, which was protesting against proposals to develop a Thermal Oxide Reprocessing Plant (THORP) at the Sellafield nuclear processing plant situated on the west coast of England in Cumbria.

The vast new facility would be three times the size of St Paul's Cathedral in London and would cost around £1.6 billion. And it was planned that it would handle fuel considered to be far more radio-active than the material being reprocessed at that time at Sellafield.

Greenpeace maintained that if this new plant was allowed to go active it would substantially increase the radioactive pollution of the Irish Sea and the nearby countryside. Radioactive discharges of dangerous Krypton gases into the air would, they feared, increase by up to 1000 per cent, and into the sea by up to 800 per cent.

Already worried about the levels of radiation contaminating the Irish Sea, Bono and the band supported the efforts being made to try to halt any further discharges of radioactive waste. They had therefore agreed to headline at the gig, and also take part in a subsequent demonstration which they hoped would focus public attention on the dangers they believed this plant posed.

The international support line-up for the gig included the UK group Big Audio Dynamite II, the American band Public Enemy (who were themselves right then on a British tour), and from Germany, the group Kraftwerk. The concert, unambiguously billed as 'Greenpeace. Stop Sellafield. The Concert', was held on 19 June at Manchester's G-Mex Arena.

It seemed apt that the biggest band on the planet should beat the drum of saving the planet but it would not be with the benefit gig – in themselves such awareness-raising events are a fairly common occurrence – that they would make the best impact.

In the hours leading up to the G-Mex gig Bono had been seen with the concert organizers in what seemed to be a series of intriguingly mysterious huddles, as if a plan was being hatched, under wraps. Then, after the show, U2 unexpectedly vanished rather rapidly, taking little or no part in the usual after-gig wind-down. The reason why became clear the following day.

Four months earlier, British Nuclear Fuels Ltd (BNFL) had given permission to a local protest group called CORE (Cumbrians Opposed to a Radioactive Environment) to hold a rally on BNFL-owned land at a specially designated site, near Sellafield's main gates. But this had been on the understanding that it would attract only a few hundred people.

The original plan, however, had subsequently mushroomed and by late May a much bigger event was anticipated. Greenpeace, with whom CORE was working in close association, had succeeded in getting U2 to agree to perform at an outdoor benefit gig on Saturday, 20 June.

Following the performance, a peaceful demonstration was going to be held, in which activists, Greenpeace officials and concerned citizens (including the band) would arrive at the main official entrance to the nuclear processing plant to make known their concerns. But these plans were successfully scuppered by BNFL at the eleventh hour.

On Tuesday, 16 June, at the High Court in London, Mr Justice May upheld British Nuclear Fuels' decision to withdraw the permission previously granted to CORE. Also at the High Court, BNFL were granted an injunction to prevent Greenpeace from staging the intended gig and/or demonstration on Sellafield property.

After the announcement of U2's participation, the scale of the event had increased considerably. Roughly 15,000 people were now expected, and BNFL had expressed concern about public safety and public order, as well as health considerations. After the injunction had been issued, a Sellafield spokesman said, 'This is not a matter of the right to free speech. It is simply a matter of an inappropriate venue, which could well lead to serious danger and harm to the public.'

Martin Forwood of CORE recalls:

Towards the end of 1991 Greenpeace were putting together a major campaign against the opening of this new reprocessing plant at Sellafield and they had all kinds of things planned. The initial plan here was that we, at CORE, as people on the ground next door to Sellafield, were to try to get permission from British Nuclear Fuels to stage an open air concert with U2 actually at Sellafield.

I was personally involved with this for months. We had meeting after meeting with BNFL and with the local police about making these arrangements and to begin with BNFL were all for it. In fact, they were quite helpful. They even said, yes you can use this car park for doing this, and you can put that on there and so on. There was a lot of enthusiasm locally and many people were really looking forward to this concert when they found out that U2 was playing.

Then, and I'm not exactly sure what happened, BNFL got cold feet. I think they realized suddenly that they were looking at maybe approaching 20,000 people all descending on Sellafield for this concert. And they pulled the plug on it. They said, 'No way are you going to do it.' I think that they were genuinely frightened about what was going to happen.

Greenpeace and ourselves said, 'Well, we're going to press ahead with it whether you like it or not.' And the next thing we knew we were served with the injunctions by BNFL that we would not carry on with the concert. That we would not be able to use any BNFL owned land, and BNFL owns a *lot* of land around Sellafield so that if they put all that off limits then there was no way you could hope to hold the concert anywhere near Sellafield.

And thirdly, we had to publically retract all the press work we had done on this and also withdraw all the invitations sent out and so on. So reluctantly we had to take the view that, okay, they had got us and we couldn't do anything about it.

Undaunted, though, the resourceful protest organizers changed tack. They quickly managed to re-schedule the gig for Friday, 19 June instead, and the venue now moved to the G-Mex Arena in Manchester.

Over 10,000 people attended the sell-out gig at which U2 put on a Zoo TV performance, with Bono dressed in his 'Fly' black leathers. On the vista of television screens, words and phrases flashed in furious rotation, from single words like 'Plutonium', 'Warhead', 'Contaminate', 'Chernobyl', to warnings such as 'Radiation Sickness', 'You Are Not Immune' and 'Nobody Is Promised A Tomorrow'.

That this was no ordinary rock gig is brought home poignantly by a local Cumbrian resident Sue Darcy who was present that night. Says Sue:

My daughter Gemma died of leukaemia. Her newspaper clippings were among those which had been put up on the walls of one of the backstage dressing rooms and Bono had been reading them. During the concert U2 played one of her favourite songs for Gemma, 'Eternal Flame' by the Bangles, and the atmosphere was untrue. It was electric.

There are a lot of families around here who are fighting about Sellafield, that the plant has caused the leukaemias but it's a lonely struggle. It makes it all worthwhile though, knowing that people like Bono and the others in U2 care and are really genuine about it.

A lot more people have come around to the way of thinking that there is something wrong here. It has enlightened people's views on Sellafield. Whereas, me, I can shout and scream about it. But when the likes of U2 stand up and say that they are fighting it, that's different. They have a big following and a lot more people sat up suddenly and took notice. They have made so many people aware of just what's going on.

I must admit I'd been a bit apprehensive at first about the gig. But I've got another daughter and she came with us and it really boosted her morale after losing her sister. It helped her to know that people in the public eye were thinking the same thing that she was.

Having succeeded in holding the gig, then, what about the planned demonstration? For some time prior to the gig, Greenpeace and CORE had meticulously reviewed their options to ascertain where they stood if plan B had to come into operation.

And so, early on Saturday morning, a smaller, but no less determined, contingent of protesters caught the authorities napping by arriving on the waters off the coast, on board the Greenpeace ship, *Solo*. From *Solo*, at 7 a.m., 100 people came ashore on to Seascale beach beside the power plant.

Martin Forwood explains, 'We got around the legal wrangles by landing them on the beach directly opposite Sellafield – this was on the strip of beach between high and low tide, which I think is owned by the Queen or something. BNFL didn't own it anyway.'

Bono, Edge, Larry Mullen and Adam Clayton were among the scores of people who washed up on the deserted stretch of sand in a small flotilla of inflatable dinghies. To drive home the point, like his bandmates, Bono wore white anti-radiation overalls, boots and a yellow fluorescent life jacket. His 'Fly' goggle dark glasses made an incongruous addition. 'We were aware of how ridiculous it was,' he admitted.

He was, however, as serious as the rest about what they were doing. U2 helped to ferry ashore a number of barrels containing contaminated silts taken from around the UK and Irish coasts. And, after lining these barrels up near the high tide mark, they posed for photographs beside them.

Giant notices were erected, bearing the words 'No Freedom of Speech Beyond This Point' and 'Warning! Radioactive Facility Sellafield'. The four band members helped erect a quantity of smaller placards mounted on poles, dotting the beach with a forest of signs proclaiming, 'Stop Sellafield'. And, for good measure, yards of yellow and black police hazard warning tape snaked all around, fluttering in the breeze.

But they hadn't finished yet. Martin Forwood reveals:

When the injunction at the High Court in London was issued, they also issued a map showing all the land that BNFL owned around Sellafield, which was a huge bonus for us because we had never actually quite known what they did and didn't own. But, by a curious omission, they had forgotten that they owned a very large car park at the next door village of Seascale. So, on that basis, it was planned that U2, having landed on the beach and done their bit, would literally walk along the beach and up into the village car park, which they did.

We had been there with a van from about four o'clock in the morning and coachloads of media people from Manchester and elsewhere arrived after the concert and people all converged down onto the beach. U2 arrived in the car park about eight o'clock and stayed there for over an hour. They were very chatty and talked to all the locals as well as having a long talk with us.

Bono was incredibly supportive – all the band members were – about what we were doing. And I think this was their way of showing that they weren't going to let the BNFL legal machine get the best of them. It was a great event and an extraordinary atmosphere on the beach on what was a very, very hot day too. Bono is very passionate about these issues. He called this place 'The Devil's back yard' which I thought was pretty good.

There was one dark moment, however, that sunny morning. This involved, among the throng of people, a man who did not support the Greenpeace/CORE initiative, as CORE activist Janine Allis-Smith recalls:

There was an incident which Bono rather took to his heart. It happened when we were all in the car park and all of a sudden this man came up to us and started effing and blinding at us.

He was asking everybody why they were there and people replied, 'Well you know, we come from London and . . .' And he cut in, saying, 'Why don't you fuck off back to London then?' Then I said about my son having had leukaemia and he said, 'Why don't you all go away and get cancer?'

I'm not a violent person. I have never slapped anybody in my life. But I just slapped out at him. It was an unfortunate moment because the police were there and they came over immediately. It was explained why it had happened – that my son has had leukaemia and everything – and the moment passed but I was still upset when U2 walked in from the beach and somebody told Bono about it. He was really quite concerned.

Martin Forwood confirms, 'If I remember rightly I think Bono commented too, "It is a pity that the television camera didn't get that." It was a really tense atmosphere after the scuffle and Bono was extremely unhappy about the incident.'

Janine Allis-Smith goes on, 'It was such a pity that it had happened because it had been just an amazing day. It was so unreal and could have been such a completely happy event.' Of Bono specifically she says, 'He wants to *know*. A lot of people are just there to show themselves off and that's enough. But he really wanted to talk to us, to listen to us.'

Janine's son recovered from his illness and, along with his brother, was left with very happy memories of U2's involvement in this campaign. Janine recalls, 'My sons had both been invited to the gig in Manchester and were allowed backstage. They had the most wonderful time, talking to the band. It was fabulous for them to be so close to the people they had posters of up on their bedroom walls.'

To news crews, Bono put forward his own view of the danger that this reprocessing plant represented and why the band were involved. He said, 'The real threat is the potential for disaster. There are certain things that we should be frightened of.' At the end of the day he admitted, 'I suppose it's a token gesture. We've given one day in a year. It's not much.' But he added that if it meant that people who were interested in the band then became focused on such important issues then it was worth it.

The beach had been festooned with photographers aiming their telephoto lenses at the band as they had posed in various positions on and around the barrels; at one point Mullen, Bono, Clayton and Edge had attempted some semaphore with little red flags for the photo call. There was news coverage of the protest all over the world, thereby scoring a triumph for Greenpeace and causing the nuclear industry some embarrassment.

The previous night during the concert Bono had spoken of the cancellation of the original event, pointing out that the whole thing had surely backfired on BNFL because it had just given far more publicity to Greenpeace and highlighted the concerns over the THORP plant more than they could have imagined.

As the dust settled over this high-profile stunt, Bono turned his attention back to music. On the day of the beach invasion, U2's new single, 'Even Better Than the Real Thing'/'Salome' had been released and by the following week it peaked at number twelve in the UK charts.

Curiously, a remix version of the self-same single released just a month later, in mid-July, charted four places higher. In America it would bottom out later in the year at number thirty-two, despite the band being, by then, one month into a new US tour.

This return visit to America commenced in August and marked the point at which U2 switched from playing indoor arenas to outdoor stadiums. Initial fears that the concept of the Zoo TV stage set would not easily translate successfully from one format to another were allayed soon enough but the band had additional concerns.

Unlike many of their major contemporary performers, U2 had resisted the temptation to accept lucrative corporate sponsorship to offset the substantial expenses of touring. Instead they carried the financial burden of mounting these massive undertakings themselves.

Their reasons were plain. U2 cherished their independence. As Bono pointed out on several occasions, not being under any company's control removed the potential risk of having to compromise their music. It was an expensive principle but one that they were prepared to adhere to, despite the strain.

The US/Canadian tour would be a colossal project. From early August to late November, U2 were scheduled to play in some of the most famous stadiums the two countries had to offer. These included the Giants Stadium in New Jersey, Montreal's Olympic Stadium, the Veterans' Stadium in Philadelphia, the Silverdome in Pontiac, the Sun Devil Stadium in Tempe, Arizona, and Los Angeles' Dodger Stadium.

At the end of August 1992 the band became only the second rock act ever, at the time, to perform at the famous giant Yankee Stadium in the Bronx, New York. (The first performer to do so had been the American singer/songwriter Billy Joel two years earlier.)

U2's stay in the Big Apple was clearly going to prove memorable. The day before these two Yankee Stadium gigs, whilst taking part in a live radio phone-in show, Bono was joined on the line by a certain 'Bill from Little Rock in Arkansas'. This turned out to be Governor Bill Clinton, the then Democratic candidate in the 1992 presidential election campaign that was entering its last stretch.

U2 had already thrown in their tuppence-worth on the political front by participating in an MTV-run nationwide campaign called 'Rock the Vote'. This was designed to challenge apathy among the younger generation towards politics and to actively urge this age group to exercise their democratic right to vote. No particular political persuasion was championed by U2; people were encouraged to study the issues and to choose for themselves.

Once Bono's caller had established that he should be addressed informally as 'Bill', the first thing Clinton did was applaud U2's involvement in 'Rock the Vote'. The trendy politician, who wore denim jeans and could play a mean saxophone, went on to make clear his appreciation of the album *The Joshua Tree*. And he particularly singled out the song 'Angel of Harlem'. Being a great Elvis Presley fan himself, Clinton loved the fact that this number had been recorded in Memphis at Sun Studios. On air, live to millions coast to coast, he declared, 'You made me feel like I had a place in rock music, even at forty-six.'

For his part, Bono reiterated that it was not his, nor U2's, intention to try to steer young voters in any specific direction. But still, on behalf of the band, the singer told Bill Clinton that he certainly *sounded* presidential.

Ringing in was a shrewd move on Clinton's part. Whilst congratulating U2, he had also skilfully slipped in his age which was youthful compared with most US presidents. And for Bono, it was a coup to have the charismatic and popular Bill Clinton take part in the show and to hear him praise the band's work. But what was interesting about this incident was the performance of both the politician and the rock star when they got down to the nitty gritty.

Bono intelligently quizzed Bill Clinton on a range of important issues, questions that were adroitly answered by the astute politician. The exercise, in Bono's case, provided further evidence that, behind the nightly on-stage dressing up and displays of decadence, there was still a deep-thinking, politically savvy individual.

Politics, of course, did infiltrate the stage when Bono, who had previously been outspoken about Ronald Reagan, began to target George Bush. During the encore at gigs he would publicly telephone the White House and ask to be connected to the President. Not surprisingly, he never managed to get past the White House switchboard operators who became suspicious of this regular caller.

As the sold-out tour bowled along, the band were to have another encounter with Bill Clinton. In November the Arkansas Governor would win the election to become America's 42nd President. But, before that, in the final few weeks of the tiring campaign trail, his and U2's paths were destined to cross in Chicago. For this latest pit stop on their respective tours, they both had suites in the city's plush Ritz Carlton Hotel.

U2 had returned to the hotel to wind down from one of their gigs and were holding a party in Bono's opulent suite of rooms when they discovered that Bill Clinton was a fellow guest at the Ritz Carlton. Emboldened by drink and in high spirits, the band spontaneously decided to ask Governor Clinton if he would like to join them and their other guests. Sadly, the idea was snuffed out when the guy who was sent along with the verbal invitation came up against a phalanx of sober-suited, formidable-looking secret service armed bodyguards who drily reminded the merry partygoer that it was 3 a.m.

Clinton heard about his enthusiastic nocturnal would-be visitor, however, the next morning and promptly took himself off to Bono's room where the aftermath of the party was pretty evident, as was the washed-out condition of the singer and his friends.

Part of Bill Clinton's trademark style has always been his air of accessibility and approachability, and he certainly seemed very much at ease relaxing with the rock stars. In time, talk turned from music to politics behind even these closed doors and surrounded by the wreckage of a party, and Bono liked what he heard.

To Bono, relations with any politician are almost automatically uneasy but that the soon-to-be most powerful man in the world intuitively seemed to recognize and respect this feeling, led him later to declare of Bill Clinton, 'He's pretty cool.'

Riding the crest of the wave, Bono awaited the next new experience as the tour rolled on. Days after the US leg had ended, U2 landed their first television special, when 'U2 – Zoo TV' was aired on Fox TV on 29 November. The programme showed four articulate guys who had lost none of the droll sense of humour that had enlivened their earliest appearances on American satellite channels as raw callow youths.

Where it counted, Bono had remained unchanged in other ways too. Onstage, as the Fly or the Mirrorball Man, he may have represented the epitome of 'assholic' attitude. And, when he was not dressed in expensive silky black clothes, smoking slender cigars, he did enjoy catching the eye by wearing his extravagant 'Fly' shiny black leathers in public too.

But offstage, Bono remained sincere in his beliefs and his dealings and was invariably still malleable with fans, to the point of finding it hard to be brusque to those who were determined to demand his time or attention.

In the same month as the tour wrapped, Bono's recorded cover version of Elvis Presley's 1962 hit 'Can't Help Falling in Love' was included in the soundtrack album for the newly released comedy *Honeymoon in Vegas*. The film, directed by Andrew Bergman and starring Nicolas Cage, James Caan and Sarah Jessica Parker, featured a crazy climax involving dozens of sky-diving Elvis look-alikes.

For U2 the last single release of the year came on 5 December with the number 'Who's Gonna Ride Your Wild Horses'/'Paint It Black' which peaked in Britain at number fourteen and at number thirty-five in America.

By the end of this phenomenal year, Zoo TV had grossed an esti-mated US$67 million. In 1992, only the Rolling Stones and New Kids on the Block had bettered this figure for a single year. U2 also attracted a slew of trophies at the Billboard Music Awards, held in December.

Although well used to lifting prizes, while the band stepped off the touring treadmill for the first quarter of 1993, Bono could scarcely have failed to be impressed by the recognition that quickly came their way as winter warmed into spring.

At London's Alexandra Palace, on 16 February, U2 collected the Best Live Act Brit Award. Eight days later at the Shrine Auditorium in Los Angeles they won the Grammy Award for the Best Rock Performance by a Duo or Group. Then, the following month, the fêted band secured International Entertainer of the Year at the annual Juno Awards held at the O'Keefe Centre in Toronto, Canada, before also making off, in May, with the accolade of Best Selling Irish Artist of the Year at the World Music Awards staged in Monte Carlo, Monaco.

Their global popularity had been plainly reaffirmed and it was a safe bet that Zoo TV was not yet exhausted. But for now the band, covered in glory, retrenched in Dublin where Bono had much to occupy his thoughts. Primarily he was deeply concerned about a project with which Ali had become involved.

Following her studies at Dublin's University College in the late 1980s, Ali had gained a degree in social science, politics and sociology. She was also the mother of two young children, and married to a man from whom she was used to being parted for long periods of time.

Now, in spring 1993, she revealed that as a couple, once again, they had had little opportunity to be with each other for over a year. 'Our communication has been erratic,' she admitted in a rare interview.

It is not an arrangement that would have suited many couples, but the Hewsons' marriage was patently strong enough to withstand such frequent and lengthy enforced separations. According to Ali, indeed, being apart only added further impetus to their relationship when they were reunited. There was never the danger of things going stale and there was always so much to catch up on.

Over the years Ali had continued to stay strictly out of the public eye. She prized her ability to go about her daily business virtually unrecognized and she had never wanted to live in the glare of the media spotlight.

'I hate being identified just as Bono's wife,' she frankly stated. And carving a very definite identity of her own was always important to her. As part of this endeavour, she participated, in her own right, in the activities of a variety of environmental organizations. And in April 1993 she agreed to join a team that was to visit Chernobyl, in the Ukraine.

In late April 1986 the world's worst civil nuclear disaster had occurred here, when there was an explosion in the number four reactor at the Chernobyl power station. It took four days before the Russians asked for assistance from Sweden and from West Germany, by which time an American satellite had picked up on the disaster and the images that were beamed to the West were telling their own horrific story.

The top of the nuclear reactor had been blown clean off. The graphite moderator of the reactor was on fire and temperatures inside reactor four at meltdown reached 4,500 degrees Fahrenheit; the flames leapt an estimated 100 feet into the air.

Two people had been killed outright, but the much greater potential danger was frighteningly obvious. Russian nuclear reactors, in those days, did not have the containment buildings that are usual in the West, designed to help prevent the release of radioactivity. Satellite images of the blazing inferno suggested that the core of the reactor was exposed and high radiation levels were already being detected in Scandinavia.

Closer to home, hundreds of thousands of people had been hastily evacuated from the state of Belarus in an attempt to reduce the danger to their health. But people are still, in the new millennium, paying with their lives because of this disaster.

Exactly seven years on from events in April 1986, Ali was now to be involved in the making of a documentary about this disaster and the true extent of its deadly legacy, called 'Black Wind, White Land – Living With Chernobyl'. She would present the documentary and it would be shown on Irish television later that year.

The work for this award-winning documentary would take Ali, in company with the documentary crew, three weeks, during which time they would stay in Belarus. The filming, moreover, took them into 'exclusion zones' – places where the radiation was highest. The dangers were numerous, from radioactive dust particles in the atmosphere to the radioactive soil beneath their feet. And there was a huge risk that the food there would be contaminated.

For this reason, the television crew travelled with their own stocks of food and water. But, once they arrived, they ran into an unlooked-for and very human dilemma. The hospitable people in this blighted region felt that it was only polite to cater for the westerners in their midst, who were trying to educate the world about the fears hanging over their daily existence. For the visitors to refuse this extended hospitality was not easy.

For Ali, to refuse would have been the same as saying that she was not prepared to chance eating what these people had to consume every day of their lives. And that was not on. She revealed later that she did accept the locals' hospitality and, she maintained, she would have to hope for the best.

It was a highly principled thing to do, but it is not hard to understand why Bono was so acutely concerned about the danger of his wife being exposed to potentially harmful levels of leaked radiation. It was always entirely her own decision whether or not to go. But it did not help Bono's nerves that the appalling state of Russian telecommunications in that region meant that there were long spells when he was unable to contact his wife by telephone.

His immersion in solo projects probably helped during this time – and the most significant of these was a new foray into writing. Bono was collaborating with Hollywood scriptwriter Nicholas Klein on a movie screenplay to be called *The Million Dollar Hotel*. The film rights would eventually be bought by Mel Gibson's film company, Icon Productions, although it would be some time before the movie went into production. Another help was that, by early 1993, the singer at last enjoyed a closer relationship with his father, Bobby Hewson.

With this break in touring, Bono had time to reflect on a few things. He knew that the introduction of alter-egos into his performances had caught the attention of the fans and the press, regardless of whether or not it had also found favour with them. And there were those who still puzzled about the meaning behind the Fly or the Mirrorball Man.

Perhaps weary of all this intellectualizing, Bono now simply stated that for the past twelve months he had dressed up as a conman on stage. And from this point on, he and the rest of U2 were disinclined to continue explaining themselves to the media.

In any event, with the caricaturing that had been most prevalent at the end of the 1980s now continuing as a result of the alter-ego characters, it is hardly surprising that Bono no longer recognized himself as he was portrayed in the press.

Bono had also joined the rest of U2 in broadening their interests with the purchase of Dublin's Clarence Hotel, part of which they would later have renovated and turned into a popular nightspot.

Music, however, eventually, inevitably, drew the four back into the studio. Initially their idea was to record an EP. But their abundance of ideas, combined with their recharged energy and enthusiasm, led to the project increasing in size until it turned into a ten-track album.

The democratic way in which the band operated in the studio seemed to be particularly highlighted for the drummer this time, who found it a liberating feeling to know that there were, as he put it, 'no rules in U2'. This meant that there was no specific pressure on any individual member to contribute a set amount.

Maybe that is why it clearly proved to be a very good experience, a time when everything gelled. The fluidity of the way in which the four worked reminded Edge of the band's collective chemistry; he called their four-man unit a 'unique collection of individuals'.

When it came to the songwriting, this time Bono was specifically aided by Edge who sat in with him during the initial creative process. The guitarist saw his role as being that of playing devil's advocate – acting as a foil for Bono's ideas – and it was a new degree of responsibility for him.

Once the basic ideas were arrived at, the development of the songs then took its more usual course. Bono can get stir-crazy after a time in the studio, however, and he paid particular tribute to Edge as a stayer. There is usually one guy in any rock band who is still going strong when all around him have wilted, and the more slow-burning one now was Edge.

Recording took place in different studios in Dublin, including Windmill Lane Studios. Situated by the docks on the south side of the River Liffey, this renowned recording home of U2 had for years been a Mecca to the band's fans, as shown by the outside walls which are famously daubed with colourful images and hand-written messages to individual band members by devotees from all over the globe.

The Factory – a studio where a portion of all U2 recordings are made – was also used. The Factory was invariably also where the band carried out their pre-tour rehearsals and this time was no exception. Having renamed the tour Zooropa '93, U2 prepared to hit the trail again; they kicked off on 9 May in Rotterdam.

The new, similarly titled *Zooropa* album was released in July, and it again checked in on both sides of the Atlantic at the top of the charts – a show of strength guaranteed to satisfy Polygram, Island Records' parent company. The month before, the company had announced their intention to sign U2 to a new, long-term deal. Press speculation as to the deal's worth ran to as high as US$200 million. But, although this was thought to be an inflated figure, the exact details would remain private.

The music press had been taken aback by the unexpected release of *Zooropa*, an album that extended the already experimental nature of *Achtung Baby*, and ventured even further into the then popular vein of heavy techno dance music. Although a stimulating experience to put together, this album had taken much out of the band.

The deadline for its completion had become so tight that it had actually overlapped the start of the tour. According to Edge, the band had had to jet back to Dublin after certain European gigs early in the itinerary to allow them to finish up in the recording studio. It was tough going for a while, but one offshoot, in addition to racking up another chart success, was that it provided extra material with which to vary their live shows.

As it happened, there was very little risk of Zooropa '93 proving to be a stale rehash of Zoo TV. For one thing, Bono had now introduced a third alter-ego, a demonic figure called MacPhisto, who would dominate the tour.

As MacPhisto, Bono appeared on stage dressed in a gold suit, worn over a lurid red shirt, with gold, glittering platform boots. His face, often split in a devilish, leering grin, was caked with white make-up, against which blood-red lipstick and heavy black eyeliner made a startling contrast. Bono's jet-black short hair was ruthlessly slicked back, and he had sprouted a pair of red stubby horns.

Bono called this new creation a 'sad, bad finale', explaining that he (MacPhisto) was weary and confused. Bass player Adam Clayton opined, 'I don't know whether Bono thought him up. I think he's been around for a long time. I just think Bono likes to wear his clothes.'

Described variously as malevolent, seedy and manic, only the character's tragic demeanour saved MacPhisto from looking frankly foolish. Yet this alter-ego baffled and provoked commentators who, clearly undeterred from having tried to analyse the Fly and the Mirrorball Man, now strove to find an intellectual fix on MacPhisto.

It was far from clear if even Bono had the answer, although sometimes he seemed to. During Zooropa '93 Bono ended gigs with 'Can't Help Falling in Love' and was fond of revealing a correlation of a kind between what he did on stage and Elvis Presley. For instance, he disclosed that the Fly outfit had been directly inspired by the sexy, figure-hugging, black soft leather that Elvis had poured himself into for his knockout 'comeback' in a celebrated 1968 television special.

MacPhisto, appearing as he did in the encore section of the shows, Bono now explained reflected the 'jaded, fat Elvis years'. The frontman empathized with this difficult period in the American legend's life and career. MacPhisto, Bono considered, represented that period when 'the derangement of stardom' took over.

As with his other alter-egos, this latest mask allowed Bono certain freedoms to interact with people whilst in character. For instance, it was as MacPhisto that Bono invited on stage a very unusual guest during one of the four Wembley Stadium gigs in London in August 1993 – author Salman Rushdie.

Rushdie had been in hiding with round-the-clock police protection, since the publication of his 1987 novel *The Satanic Verses*. With this book he had been accused of causing monumental offence to those of the Islamic faith – offence that had resulted in the then leader of Iran, the Ayatollah Khomeini, issuing a fatwah (death warrant) on the writer.

Salman Rushdie's public appearances were therefore extremely rare and had to be made, of necessity, without any warning. Salman had made a surprise visit backstage at U2's Earl's Court London show the previous year and in the intervening time the band and he had managed to keep in touch.

Although it had proved potentially hazardous to people's safety to even be associated with the hunted author, Bono spoke for the entire band when he stressed, in general, the importance of holding firm to the fundamental right of freedom of speech.

At Wembley Stadium Bono first went through a charade of trying to raise Salman Rushdie on the telephone when, as planned but to the amazement of the 72,000-strong crowd, the writer strolled on with a mobile phone held to his ear. It was a brief appearance during which Rushdie, looking at Bono rigged out as MacPhisto, told the audience, 'Real devils don't wear horns.' In character, Bono replied, 'Ladies and gentlemen, I bow to the superior man.'

The Wembley audience gave the controversial writer a hugely warm reception. And Salman Rushdie expressed his appreciation by stating soon afterwards in the press, 'I owe U2 a debt of gratitude for the gesture of solidarity and friendship.'

The four Wembley Stadium gigs left Bono hoarse, but also pleased to see the performances described as having been truly spectacular. To celebrate, after the final gig on 21 August, U2 held a post Wembley gig lavish party at London's Regent Hotel, which began around 2 a.m. Bono may have begun the night drinking beer, only to switch to whisky, but his seemingly inexhaustible energy kept him going for hours.

Zooropa '93, never dull, was not just a tour dominated by showbiz flash, however. It was also punctuated with hard political and social home truths. Bono recognized that the appetite for issue-conscious, slogan-waving rock stars was fast waning, and he called comedians the new prophets of the 1990s. But this did not stop U2 from pressing home the desperate situation of people in the war-torn city of Sarajevo, a conflict which was already being extensively covered in the nation's television and radio news.

Using their featured satellite technology on stage, the band brought the suffering in this region into stark relief. The faces of ordinary Bosnians were shown on the giant video walls during specially set up live link-ups in which Bono and these people could talk to one another.

Sarajevo citizens, be they Serb, Croat or Muslim, spoke directly to the stunned stadium crowds live and they told of organized rape and systematic torture. They were show-stopping moments, but the fall-out from them was unpredictable. The extreme levels of despair and resignation being beamed long-distance to the gigs could sometimes leave a lead weight in the stomach of those audience members who had come along to have a good night out, and for the band.

Edge described what they beamed into their gigs as being a world away from the – to some extent – sanitized reporting seen on regular news bulletins. This, he said, was 'raw, live, unedited and at times almost unbearable'.

Bono, too, was sometimes left so affected by the words of the people living in homes whose walls were pockmarked by shells and gunfire, that it was understandably difficult for him to somehow switch back to enjoying the gig and moving on.

This practice, which practically only U2 would have thought

of staging, was both applauded and attacked by media critics. Whilst no one doubted U2's sincerity in highlighting their plight, some commentators wondered about the wisdom of using rock gigs to shove political issues of human suffering in people's faces.

The European leg of the tour ended in late August and the world tour would not resume until November in Australia. In the meantime, Bono dived with gusto into another solo project that resulted in him recording a duet with Frank Sinatra.

Bono admired the New Jersey-born superstar and, over the years, he had attended a handful of Sinatra's concerts. One of the most memorable occasions had happened about five years earlier when U2 had been on the cover of *Time* magazine and had been the toast of the town.

In a Las Vegas venue, U2 (as guests of the singer) had been positioned at a privileged table close to the stage. Bono remembered with evident glee that Sinatra had singled U2 out, directing that the spotlight be shone on them, and had drawn the audience's attention to them.

Somewhat self-consciously, the four had obligingly stood up to acknowledge the crowd. Bono delightedly revealed how Frank Sinatra, who usually preferred to perform dressed in a dinner suit and bow tie, had gently mocked the younger musicians' less formal appearance by declaring from the stage, 'Well, you didn't spend a dime on clothes!' Afterwards they had all met up backstage.

Clearly Bono admired the former member of the once notorious 'Rat Pack', both as a singer and as a professional entertainer. Unsurprisingly, then, he felt honoured when in 1993 Frank Sinatra asked if he would record a song with him for his new album.

The song Sinatra picked was the Cole Porter classic 'I've Got You Under My Skin'. At thirty-three, Bono was less than half the age of the then seventy-eight-year-old and their singing styles inescapably illuminated that generational gap. As Bono would point out about the singer whom the world nicknamed 'Ol' Blue Eyes', 'He's had fifty years working on phrasing!'

In the end, Bono figured that he personally ought to approach the song by striving to lock into its atmospheric quality, rather than trying to emulate the crooner's style. It may have seemed an incongruous pairing but it worked, although Bono's residual nerves about recording with the veteran showman made him glad that they did not actually record the song together in the same studio.

'I've Got You Under My Skin' formed part of Frank Sinatra's album *Duets*. It was also the B side of U2's new single titled 'Stay (Faraway, So Close)' which, reaching number four in the UK charts, when it was released on 4 December 1993, was the first U2 single in the space of a year.

By the time of the new single's release, U2 had returned from the last leg of their world tour which had commenced in Australia in mid-November and ended about a month later in Japan. It brought to a close, an astonishing, two-year-long extravaganza that had blown apart the traditional expectations of stadium entertainment.

The unpredictable nature of much of what they had done over this two-year period had appealed to Bono, who likes the way in which the band feel that they never know just what is around the corner. That way, he maintains, life stays interesting – something that is essential to all the band members.

That said, not every unexpected event had been welcome. During the band's recent Australian stint, it was more than just the usual strain, synonymous with living constantly on the road, that had clouded matters. The band had come close to a minor crisis.

Adam Clayton still revelled in leading the rock star life. Although the rest of the band had, at times, held differing views on that, the bass player's choice as to how to live his private life had not affected the band professionally. But then, in December, Clayton had missed one of U2's gigs at a Sydney football stadium.

For a time this non-appearance would be marked down vaguely as having been due to an unspecified over-indulgence. But it would come to be assumed to have been drink. That night Adam Clayton's roadie, Stuart Morgan, stood in for him and played bass guitar.

Obviously, Adam Clayton's absence from the line-up was noted immediately but the band closed ranks. They would not give this story, or any talk of there being a problem in the band, any airtime at all.

There might very well have been a real crisis had this not proved to be a single event. Edge certainly ranked it as a bad moment but, like Larry Mullen and Bono, he was able to see it in its proper context. After all, U2 were very different from some other rock bands. Instead of turning on a band member who had temporarily gone off the rails, they rallied supportively around him.

Generally speaking, Bono, Edge and Larry Mullen preferred not to discuss this moment publicly. But Edge did reveal that he would like to think that if any one of the band developed any sort of a problem, that the others would be there to help him pull through. Mullen meanwhile admitted, 'We just thought, okay, the guy's having a problem. Let's see what we can do.'

Whilst it must have been gratifying to find that his friends were there for him, it would be Adam Clayton himself who ultimately took the decision to go on the wagon. He has not had a drink since 1996.

In the intervening years between that incident in Sydney and his decision to stop drinking, Clayton would come to the conclusion that drinking was denying him the chance to lead a completely fulfilling life. Years later, he admitted about his latter years as a drinker, 'I was living a more isolated life. I was paranoid, uncomfortable.'

At the end of 1993, with the Zoo TV tour finally at an end, Adam Clayton reckoned that it had been a madcap return to the limelight for U2, during which reality and fantasy had, at times, got mixed up big-time. Only the challenging creativity and excitement had made it possible for the band to sustain the trip. It would certainly have been a hard act to follow and they had no intention of trying. Even so, by the bass player's own estimation, it would take U2 a good twelve months to recover.

CHAPTER 11

Chameleon

THREE YEARS AWAY from frontline performing can be enough to kill even the most popular band stone dead, and U2 had never intended their absence to last so long. Yet 1994 to 1997 were by no means wilderness years; rather this was a time when they had a chance to take a breath and focus on other aspects of life.

As the four friends scattered, Bono made the most of the opportunity to concentrate his attention on his wife and two daughters. For someone who was so loquacious on practically every other topic, he had always revealed precious little about his private world. All that was obvious about the singer was that, when he was not involved in recording or performing music, he was a homebody.

During this early part of 1994 it also became clear that he was visibly more relaxed on those occasions when he socialized in public around Dublin's pubs or – as became increasingly more likely – in the band's own dance club, called The Kitchen, which they had recently opened in the basement of the Clarence Hotel. This trendy, popular nightspot provided them with the perfect place in which to live it up, or alternatively, unwind, whilst they were in their own home town.

Bono never seemed content, however, to hover about in the

same place indefinitely. So at the end of February he headed to New York. He had dropped in on that city once already this year when, six weeks previously, he had inducted Bob Marley, the Jamaican-born reggae star who had died in 1981 and of whom U2 had been staunch fans, into the Rock and Roll Hall of Fame at a ceremony held at the Waldorf Astoria.

This time Bono was in New York City with the rest of the band, to collect, on 1 March, the Grammy Award for Best Alternative Music Album for *Zooropa*. In his acceptance speech he pledged, 'We shall continue to abuse our position and fuck up the mainstream.'

That said, at this same ceremony the singer would play his part in celebrating the achievements of one of the world's most stalwart mainstream performers when he presented Frank Sinatra with the Living Legend honour. For decades rumours had circulated suggesting a connection between Sinatra and the Mafia in America. Yet this hard man aura had only served to enhance Sinatra's standing, giving him an extra dark edge.

In his lengthy speech introducing the crooner-cum-film star on stage, Bono drew comparisons between some rock stars who *played* at having 'attitude' and Frank Sinatra who exhibited the real thing. Bono ended his big build-up by urging a thunderous reception for the singer with the words, 'He is a man as recognizable as the Statue of Liberty and living proof that God is a Catholic!'

In the ephemeral world of popular music, U2's longevity was becoming increasingly recognized, in terms of the prestigious accolades being afforded them. Adding to the shower of annual trophies, on 25 May at London's Grosvenor House Hotel, accompanied by Edge, Bono proudly accepted the Ivor Novello Special Award for International Achievement.

After that night, for the next several months Bono bowed out of the public eye, slipping back behind the curtain into home life. The luxury of being able to relax allowed him the scope to indulge his penchant for dabbling in interests outside music, such as film. He already had *The Million Dollar Hotel* project in play, although there were still no moves to start production on the movie. And he had also entered the arena of writing film theme music.

On 9 April 1994 the single 'In The Name of the Father, co-written by Bono and his friend Gavin Friday, had debuted at its UK peak of number forty-six. Whilst not ranking as a particularly impressive chart performance, it was an extremely striking theme tune for a memorable film of the same name. Having premiered in December 1993 and been directed by fellow Dubliner, Jim Sheridan, it starred the inimitable Daniel Day-Lewis as Gerry Conlon, one of the 'Guildford Four', whose real-life story became known as one of Britain's biggest miscarriages of justice.

It was a chilling movie concerning a devastating moment when the terrorism of an embattled Northern Ireland moved onto the British mainland, and grave imperfections in the British justice system were exposed. To complement the stark subject matter, Bono and Gavin Friday composed a suitably powerful number in which the lyrics are spoken in an edgy Irish monotone against a build-up of discordant sound. At its crescendo, it vividly evoked the carnage of a bomb blast that left a busy public house barely recognizable and, amid the wreckage, the torn and bloodied limbs of innocent human beings.

Bono would follow this up by composing the theme tune to another international blockbuster movie the next year. But before that, an insight into his abiding interest in the film world came when in mid-September 1994 he forked out a reported $56,000 for a costume worn by Charlie Chaplin in the black and white 1940 movie *The Great Dictator* – an Oscar-nominated satire on Adolf Hitler for which Chaplin had also been writer/director. Bono subsequently loaned the costume to Dublin's Hard Rock Café for exhibition.

Bono's musical collaborations continued to evolve in 1995 when, along with Christy Moore, one of Ireland's most respected musicians, he co-wrote a new Irish anthem called 'North and South of the River'. Expressing regret for the past and hope for a reconciliation, the song was an emotional plea for a sustainable peace in their divided country. It was recorded by Christy Moore. But Bono surprised many by revealing that, at least in the immediate future, he had no intention of performing this number live with U2.

Right then, he was still conscious that the elevated status which U2 enjoyed in the world could seriously irritate some people in Ireland. When pressed as to why the band would not sing the folksy, political ballad 'North and South of the River' live, Bono replied, 'Because if we did, it would induce projectile vomit from all quarters.'

Having suffered considerable flak in the past for grandstanding about such issues, Bono had come to the conclusion that there were smarter ways of addressing things.

Come springtime 1995, the band then reconvened specifically to record a number for inclusion in the film soundtrack for *Batman Forever* called 'Hold Me, Thrill Me, Kiss Me, Kill Me'. Backed by the theme from the film and released on 17 June 1995, it reached number two in the UK singles chart and number sixteen in America. And it marked the moment when U2 quietly returned to the studio. It was, though, to involve themselves in a very different project.

Having worked with Brian Eno for years in the capacity of producer, the band had long wanted to find a project in which they could collaborate in full; in other words, they wanted Eno to become like a temporary unofficial fifth member of U2.

These plans took shape when the five devoted five weeks in early summer to recording sessions in Dublin on an album to be called *Original Soundtracks 1*. A fortnight during the previous November at London's Westside Studio had kick-started the work that would bring in other guest contributors, including the opera star Luciano Pavarotti, London-based Scottish disc jockey Howie B., and Japanese singer Holi.

This experimental soundtrack music would be made under the collective name of Passengers. The album provided Bono and the others with a vehicle to make music with whomever they wished – their imagination was the only limit.

The hit single to emerge from the work would be the number on which Bono duetted with the Italian tenor. Called 'Miss Sarajevo', this track had evolved out of a short documentary, made some two years earlier and produced by Bono, which had focused on life in the battle-weary Bosnian capital.

The documentary had highlighted the ways in which music had assisted the young people cowering in bomb shelters to blot out the threat of death. Bono had been astounded and moved to discover that discos had taken place in such circumstances, that television sets had brought MTV to them, and that they had played records, among them U2 records, to drown out the noise of gunfire.

With the bit between his teeth, Luciano Pavarotti had proved to be even more tireless than Bono, and the frontman had found himself bombarded with daily personal telephone calls and messages urging him to write a song for the opera star. The outcome had been 'Miss Sarajevo'.

It came as no surprise either when Pavarotti invited Bono to premiere this song with him at the annual massive outdoor concert called 'Pavarotti and Friends' held on 12 September at Novi Sad Park in the opera star's home town of Modena to raise money for the Bosnia War Child charity.

U2's agreement to take part in this event landed them the five-star treatment. In an over-the-top display of pomp, the band were met on arrival at the airport by a fleet of spectacular, chauffeur-driven, white stretch limousines, ready to whisk them to Pavarotti's lavish home. This was a level of pampering that, despite himself, impressed Bono.

However, not everyone was impressed when *Original Soundtracks 1* was released on 18 November 1995. It peaked at number twelve in Britain but petered out at a lowly number seventy-six in the States. Critically speaking, the album was broadly ignored.

It was baffling to some. To call it a soundtrack album was a misnomer, since there was no movie. Bono felt that, atmospherically, it constituted late night listening. He also acknowledged that the processed studio techniques that had been used to distort the instruments' sound might not find universal favour. It was an experimental album, work on which he personally had considered to be stimulating. But, in all honesty, he conceded that it could be construed as a 'selfish' record.

Illustrating the spirit of individual free speech that existed strongly within U2, Larry Mullen broke ranks to express his dislike of the album. On more than one occasion he roundly condemned the entire exercise as having been an act of pure self-indulgence.

On the same day as *Original Soundtracks* 1 was released, the single 'Golden Eye', sung by Tina Turner, entered the UK charts at number ten. Co-written by Bono and Edge, it was the theme song to the new James Bond movie of the same name which premiered that month, starring Pierce Brosnan and Sean Bean.

By now Bono's work as a lyricist had earned him official entry into the literary world. The year 1995 had been designated the UK Year of Literature and Writing and he had been invited to become one of over thirty patrons, including the former Labour Prime Minister Lord Callaghan, the renowned playwright Arthur Miller and Salman Rushdie among others.

There had been a series of events – poetry recitals, seminars, debates, etc. – staged to promote literature and at the same time to raise awareness of human rights. Bono had been asked to be a guest speaker at one of these gatherings, held one evening in mid-October at the Swansea Grand Theatre, since lyric writing had newly been put on the same footing as poetry and fiction.

Bono arrived by chartered plane, sporting a new look. He had grown a beard and favoured a severely cropped hairstyle, which he initially hid under an unflattering brown tweed flat cap. The Grand Theatre has a 1,200-seat capacity, but this proved to be insufficient when a small army of U2 fans converged on the event, swelling the numbers inside and leaving hundreds hanging around outside.

Bono made his entrance centre stage for a ninety-minute spot to a blaze of popping flash bulbs, deafening applause and rafter-rattling cheers. Yet, despite this warm welcome, in distinguished company, he seemed at first to be a little ill at ease.

His 45-minute talk was followed by a 45-minute question and answer session. Friendliness and a sharp wit emanated from the frontman in the latter section. And, once he settled into it, his talk was watermarked with typical Bono bluntness.

Whilst at this event, Bono also gave his first media interviews in two and a half years. The music newspaper *NME* reported that part of the singer's talk included references to most rock and roll lyrics being based on the less than intellectual premise, 'I want to shag you'. The tenor of the talk rose above this for the main part, but it did show that Bono was not prepared to temper his words to befit a sober literary gathering.

Weeks later, on 23 November, Bono's outspokenness caused further shockwaves. At the MTV Europe Awards ceremony held at Le Zenith in Paris, where U2 had picked up the Best Group Award, he added his voice to the already widespread international condemnation of nuclear bomb tests being carried out by France in the South Pacific.

His scathing verbal attack on French President Jacques Chirac had segued startlingly from a speech that had begun innocuously enough. In an abruptly phrased outburst that would be widely reported Bono rapped out, 'What a city. What a night. What a crowd! What a bomb! What a mistake! What a wanker you have for President! What are you gonna do about it?'

Just as Bono had once again displayed his opposition to war, and as 'Miss Sarajevo'/'One (live)', credited to Passengers, lodged at number six in the British charts on 2 December, the three and a half year war in Bosnia was finally about to end.

As 1995 drew to an end, this development allowed Bono to see in the new year in Sarajevo as a guest of the Bosnian government and so he and Ali arrived on 30 December aboard a United Nations aid flight from the Croatian capital Zagreb.

Originally it had been intended as a private visit. But then Bono called a news conference, provoking a stampede of press, photographers and news camera crews. The Bosnian Foreign Minister, Mohammed Sacirbey, sat beside the singer as he expressed his respect and admiration for the enduring courage of Sarajevo's people.

'If rock and roll music means anything, it's some kind of liberation,' said Bono to the assembled journalists and foreign correspondents.

He also took part in a telephone interview for Bosnian state television during which he claimed an affinity with the people there. Ireland, too, was a small and deeply divided country.

On a lighter note, he dubbed himself 'a tourist with a conscience'. As such, he went walkabout around the city, shadowed by the international media posse every step of the way. Before Bono left Bosnia Herzegovina he promised that the next time, he would return with U2 to perform. That prospect was some time distant, and indeed it was very nearly made impossible by a terrifying experience which the singer suffered just two weeks into the new year.

Having been a guest of Chris Blackwell at the Pink Sands (one of the hotel resorts owned by the Island Records founder in Jamaica), Bono with Blackwell was on board a private seaplane which, soon after taking off from Montego Bay, came under machine-gun fire.

Jamaican police had incorrectly identified it as a plane about which they had received an anonymous tip and which was said to be carrying drugs. It was a case of mistaken identity, but the startled pilot had to make an alarming emergency landing. The situation was swiftly clarified and no one had been hurt, but the bullets lodged in a spray in the plane's side bore gruesome testimony as to how close they had all come to disaster.

Putting this hair-raising incident behind him, Bono returned home in the knowledge that he had two major projects to interest him in 1996. Firstly, filming was finally about to commence on *The Million Dollar Hotel* – principal photography would begin in Los Angeles under German film director Wim Wenders. It had been a long wait between having the germ of an idea for a movie script, to the movie actually going into production.

Bono had experienced a little of Los Angeles' sordid underbelly during a U2 visit there years before, when a young woman took a dive out of a high-rise apartment window, to meet a hideous death on the cold concrete sidewalk below. This single incident had provided the inspiration from which a film script had evolved in the hands of himself, Nicholas Klein and others.

It told the story of an FBI investigation into the death of a billionaire's son in a seedy downtown hotel, and raised the question, was it murder of suicide? *The Million Dollar Hotel*, starring Mel Gibson, Milla Jovovich, Amanda Plummer, Jimmy Smits and Jeremy Davies, would eventually go on general release in 2000.

U2's extended break was now coming to an end. In many ways, it had been a good time for everyone. Bono and Edge, with their respective families, had teamed up for a spell in Nice, in France. And part of this time had been given over to listening to a wide variety of sounds.

Like the guitarist, Bono was curious about the hip hop techno style that was so much in vogue. Thinking of U2's next direction, they welcomed the notion once more of being adventurous. Larry Mullen and Adam Clayton agreed. Indeed, Clayton had taken off the previous year to America to immerse himself in studying music, particularly bass guitar playing techniques.

Finally, work on U2's next album got underway. Some foundations had been laid a few months earlier during a brief spell in London with two songs (from the ultimately twelve-track album) called 'Wake Up Dead Man' and 'If You Wear That Velvet Dress'. But labour in earnest began in February 1996. At this stage they intended to release the album later that year.

There had been a change of personnel on the production side and Brian Eno would not be involved with this album. By mutual consent he and the band had parted company for the moment. In Eno's place came the record engineer Flood, who had worked on *Zooropa*, and in the studio the band also welcomed the assistance of disc jockey/producer Howie B., whom U2 had first met whilst working on the Passengers project.

Their determination not to set any parameters had always been a U2 hallmark and, as their 1990s' musical style forged its own path, Bono reiterated that it was not simply about maintaining success. 'Staying relevant is the big challenge,' he declared. The new blood in the recording studio could only aid this.

Recording would ultimately take place in three Dublin studios – Hanover Studios, Windmill Lane and The Works, with the band relocating around spring to South Beach Studios in Miami, Florida. It felt right, and on 9 May the band were confident enough to announce plans for a massive world tour that would commence the following year, in spring 1997.

Approaching summer 1996 it was a nostalgic time for U2 for it marked twenty years since the four had first got together as a result of that now famous notice on the Mount Temple High School bulletin board. They had come an almost unimaginable distance in that time.

Like his bandmates, Bono had not forgotten that one of the people who had been instrumental in providing the fledgling foursome with much-needed support had been *Hot Press* journalist Bill Graham. It was especially sad, then, just as they were happily wallowing in memories of those early days, they heard the shock news that Bill Graham had died suddenly at home. The band immediately flew from America to Dublin to attend the funeral, very subdued at having lost another valued friend.

When work resumed on the new album it refused to click into place straight away and it gradually became clear that it was not going to be on schedule. Indeed, by August, the release date had to be officially bumped to the following March. There can't have been many happy faces around the record company offices at the prospect of being forced to miss out on the massive Christmas market, but it was unavoidable.

It was difficult to get a fix, too, on what to expect from a band with an established reputation for springing surprises. And that autumn Bono did nothing to clarify the picture when, talking to journalists about the new album that was slowly taking shape, he described it as 'a mixed up kid' of a record.

When U2 were finally ready to step into the spotlight on 12 February 1997, their New York City press conference was held in, of all places, a K-Mart store in Manhattan's East Village. There, they announced details of their world tour, to be called Pop Mart, which would start on 25 April and would travel to eighty cities in twenty countries.

Dressed in his habitual black with a purple shirt and tie and yellow tinted shades, and with a gold earring in either ear, Bono looked an unlikely shopper. In addition to answering a barrage of questions from the lively battery of press and media who had flocked to K-Mart, at one point he negotiated his way about the store singing the song 'Holy Joe' whilst pushing a shopping trolley.

He talked of U2 taking 'the supermarket on the road' which, at the time, was probably totally incomprehensible to the press pack. Bono himself admitted that he could not now recall where the idea had sprung from to announce their new tour in a store, but it had seemed inspired at the time.

Three days later it also proved to have been an inspired choice to make the first single release from the album, the number 'Discotheque'/'Holy Joe', for, while it stopped at number ten in America, it entered the British charts at number one.

Even more success came exactly one month later when, on 15 March, the album *Pop* entered the charts at the top in both the UK and (a week later) in the US. It similarly debuted at number one in a further twenty-six countries. In America, in its first week on sale, *Pop* sold close on 350,000 copies.

When compared statistically with the first week's sales figures for *Achtung Baby* and *Zooropa* it was estimated that the new album would match the five million copies sold mark. A spokesman for the record label even anticipated a potential figure of nearly double that. But, in any event, it more than soothed the ruffled feathers caused the year before at missing out on the lucrative Yuletide market.

It had been a project so long in the making that it felt strange once it had been completed. Adam Clayton, in particular, felt that a part of his reason for getting up every day had suddenly been taken away. The end product, though, received a mixed response.

Pop did attract some excellent reviews, but the album was generally considered to be largely musically distant from the band's more popular material. Edge concurred that, on some tracks, the band had ventured further than ever before away from their once characteristic style.

Meanwhile, Larry Mullen warned, 'It's easy to lose what's special about a band through technology.' And years later he also admitted, with brutal candour, that he had had 'no fucking idea' what the album *Pop* had been about.

For some fans it was a relief that rumours about the album being totally dominated by electronic dance music had proved to be unfounded. Two or three of the tracks, in fact, were examples of U2's straightest songwriting in years. Bono described the songs on their new album as still, after all these years, being of faith and of doubt, reiterating that there remained a darkness in their material.

Undoubtedly, the song on this album that commanded Bono's

closest affection was 'Mofo', a number in which, he revealed, he talked to his dead mother. The singer had already remarked that the album had been intended to appeal to people on a very personal level, making them feel as if it related to their own lives.

In a strange, almost sad, sense, Bono believed that this one track 'Mofo' summed up his entire life and his reasons for being in music – an admission that he confessed disturbed him. He also, however, credited this song with giving him the impetus to get back to live performance.

All too soon the opportunity to do just that arrived. The Pop Mart world tour kicked off on Friday, 25 April 1997, at the 38,000-seater Sam Boyd Silver Bowl Stadium in Las Vegas. Arriving in this world-famous gambling mecca, Bono gave the ever-present camera crews a welcome soundbite when he commented that casinos had taken over from cathedrals, meaning that – for a lot of people – money was now God.

Money issues certainly preoccupied some commentators. Firstly, there was the surprise news that ticket sales for the tour were initially very uneven. Many shows *were* sold out and in some cities extra dates had to be added to cope with demand. But some newspaper reports also revealed ticket sales of only 20,000 in some places. It was a situation that sorted itself out when, within weeks, ticket sales (at US$50 each) had mushroomed to reach a healthy two million plus mark.

Then there was the question of the astronomical sum of money it was going to take to keep this spectacular show on the road. One source estimated that it would cost U2 a staggering US$250,000 a day to mount. The tour as a whole, with merchandizing sales, was expected to gross in the region of US$400 million. And once again the band refused to accept sponsorship.

Bono now flatly rejected the idea that this stance was a question of U2 taking the moral high ground. Provided they would not have to kiss ass for the privilege, he maintained that U2 would, in all likelihood, happily accept such an injection of cash. In any event, as the singer baldly pointed out, they had all raked in sufficient riches over the years to be able to shoulder the responsibility – one of the perks of being, as he put it, 'stinko'.

It wasn't hard to understand why Pop Mart was such a costly outing. There was a general malaise in the music industry at this time, and Bono believed that this came down in good part to the record business having become lethargic and dull. In setting out to outdo their own extravagance in the Zoo TV Tour, U2 made sure that this accusation could never be levelled at them.

Gaudy, garish and kitsch – these descriptions all fitted. But the Pop Mart stage set was also an eye-popping visual feast. It involved the world's largest video screen, measuring 150 feet by 50 feet, operated by 21,000 circuit boards. And stage props included a 100-foot golden arch, and a 12-foot wide illuminated stuffed olive impaled on a 100-foot toothpick. There were also 1,000 lighting fixtures, a plexiglass dance floor, a motorized 35-foot lemon that changed shape into a disco mirrorball and 100 strobe lights.

Assembling this took 250 touring personnel, who were joined at each venue by a further, locally employed 200 technicians and other helpers. And the set itself took thirty-six hours to erect. When the entire touring cavalcade arrived in town, they did so aboard seventy-five trucks, sixteen buses and two planes.

Sometimes Bono questioned why they felt this need to provide a mind-boggling spectacle. Larry Mullen bluntly nutshelled the reason by stating that, in a world obsessed with visual imagery, the days of expecting fans to be content with just four guys standing on stage, playing their instruments and singing, were dead and gone. When the predictable intellectualizing as to U2's motives started up, the drummer again doused this by stating that the band's message remained the same, only the presentation had altered.

That the presentation might, at first, be problematic, soon became evident. Greeting the opening of the tour, in conjunction with press stories of a sluggish start in places to ticket sales, came the headline next day, 'Pop Mart tour kicks off with a thud!'

The tour's opening 130-minute set at the Sam Boyd Silver Bowl Stadium in Las Vegas would come to be widely regarded as having been something of a shambles. Some critics put it down to first night jitters.

The songs were an amalgam of the band's 1980s classics and the new material from *Pop*, some of which numbers went without a hitch. However, in the case of other new songs, agreeing on the tempo seemed to be hard. Jon Pareles of the *New York Times* noted in his review of the gig that when it came to performing 'Staring at the Sun', 'after one attempt fell apart, Bono announced that the group was having "a little family row"'.

The 'family' was only too acutely aware of the sickening sensation of fear that was gripping the stage. Adam Clayton later revealed that he had been sweating so much with nervous anxiety that it had not only inhibited his ability to perform properly, but that he was left feeling physically drained by the experience.

The day after the gig, on 26 April, an ABC TV special titled 'U2: A Year in Pop' was aired, only to become the lowest ever rated non-political primetime show in American television history. In Britain that same day, the new single 'Staring at the Sun', backed by 'North and South of the River', was released, making number three, but it stalled at twenty-six in America.

Bono later agreed that the band took some time to settle in to the tour, partly because they had needed time to get to grips with the new gadgetry. He said, 'We'd just taken possession of all that cosmic junk about a week before and we didn't know how it worked.'

One month on, after a handful or so more gigs in which they ironed out their teething problems, U2 really hit their stride. Bono recognized the change at once and announced that they were beginning to turn in, 'the most transcendent shows we've played for ten years'.

One thing less to bother with throughout this tour, were

alter-egos. Not all of Bono's former stage personas had ever been foisted on to American audiences, but now role-playing was a thing of the past and the U2 show was, as Bono phrased it, 'an irony-free zone'. Fun and funky were the new watchwords.

Ultimately, still, Adam Clayton would wonder whether the concept of Pop Mart had truly found its mark with American audiences. In retrospect he came to the conclusion, 'Whatever we were playing around with, it wasn't touching the right buttons.'

Having headed from Las Vegas first to San Diego then Denver at the beginning of May, U2 arrived in Kansas City halfway through this month. There for a two-night engagement, they caused chaos whilst shooting outdoor street scenes for a new video when they unwittingly managed to disrupt the traffic flow on three interconnecting routes.

The month of May bowed out with a gig at the Giants Stadium in New York. But, before U2 quit this city, on 7 June, they temporarily jumped off the Pop Mart Tour bus to make a five-song set guest appearance at the Tibetan Freedom Concert, held at Downing Stadium on Randall's Island.

It was not always Bono who took the lead in speaking out. At this event, Larry Mullen unequivocally drove home in backstage interviews that fighting for the rights of human rights prisoners around the world had always been important to U2, even when taking such stands had become unfashionable.

U2 had deliberately made their participation in this gig quite low-key, having turned down the chance to headline at it and being content to put in a daytime appearance. For Edge, this was the way to go because he had been increasingly concerned that U2 was in danger of being overwhelmingly associated with benefit gigs, to the detriment of their career as a rock band. He didn't want them to be viewed as the 'Batman and Robin' of the rock scene!

Larry Mullen joined Bono as a guest on the top-rated CBS-TV network *David Letterman Show*, days after U2's appearance at the Tibetan Freedom gig. By this time the tour had taken the band to

Canada, then back to America, where the first leg of Pop Mart ended on 1 July at the Foxboro Stadium in Boston.

Seventeen days separated this and the European dates commencing at the Feyernoord Stadium in Rotterdam, Holland; over two consecutive nights there U2 played to a combined audience of 91,000. On 2 August came the single 'Last Night on Earth'/'Pop Muzik' (the making of the video for the A side had caused the traffic chaos in Kansas). Again, its number ten UK performance, greatly bettered the number fifty-seven placing in the States. But, for now, Bono paid more attention to a number of significant upcoming gigs.

The first landmark event this trip occurred on 12 August 1997 when U2 played their debut gig in Poland before a capacity 52,000-strong crowd at the Tor Sluzewekky in Warsaw. Days later, Bono carried off, on the band's behalf, the Best International Act prize at the Comet Awards in Cologne, Germany. After this confidence-booster, they headed off to Britain for two nights at London's Wembley Stadium.

The following week, after an absence of over ten years, U2 flew in to perform in Northern Ireland. Stepping off the plane at Belfast International Airport, they were met by a sizeable press corp.

Bono had been greatly anticipating this gig, to be held at the Botanic Gardens in Belfast on 26 August, but he was also careful not to plunge into the volatile political debate. There was an IRA ceasefire in place which, like most of his countrymen, he was very pleased about. But, when asked by journalists to comment on the current situation, he was more circumspect than some might have expected him to be.

Bono was very aware that the issues in the province were immensely complex. Hailing as he did from southern Ireland, he admitted that he could not begin to fully understand the difficulties faced by people in the north. He therefore, wisely, confined himself to expressing the hope that both communities would welcome the band and enjoy the gig. 'We feel a part of both communities,' he stressed. The gig itself ranked as a highlight for band and crowd alike. Bono ended it with the words, 'Goodnight Belfast. We'll never forget tonight.'

Ironically, it was, in fact, two gigs in the singer's home town that temporarily upset the apple cart. The last two days of August had been designated as Dublin dates. But, as soon as this had been announced, a row erupted over the choice of venue.

The rumpus was occasioned when a small group of local residents objected to the band playing their gigs at Lansdowne Road Rugby Stadium. These objections had initially been upheld by a High Court ruling that had banned the performances. Subsequently, though, this ruling was overturned by Ireland's Supreme Court, which allowed the concerts to go ahead.

It was an unfortunate state of affairs, and Bono had not been entirely happy at U2 having had to take recourse to the Supreme Court to fight the earlier decision. But he believed that stadiums were built to serve the community, and music, he felt, had no less a right to be played there than sport.

He was also, uncomfortably, of the opinion that people may have been laughing at U2 over this conflict. Whereas Larry Mullen managed to take the whole episode in a lighter vein, Bono felt a shade embarrassed by it all.

Winning the right to be able to play the Lansdowne Road Rugby Stadium gigs had been a matter of principle. But it seemed even more worthwhile when the 40,000 strong crowd at each of the two gigs gave the band a hugely warm welcome home, bowling them along to an even bigger high.

There was a gig still to come that, more than any other, Bono had been champing at the bit to secure the chance of performing. But, before that, as he and the others headed back into Europe, two more appearances were particularly noteworthy. One was held on 20 September at the Festa Dell Unita Corregio in Reggio Emilia, Italy, when the band were watched by over 150,000 people. And the second was ten days later, when U2 completed the European leg of Pop Mart by performing their first ever gig in Israel at Tel Aviv's Hayarkon Park.

Indubitably, however, the real highlight for Bono was a concert sandwiched between these two gigs; on Tuesday, 23 September 1997, U2 performed at the Kosovo Olympic Stadium in Sarajevo.

It was the fulfilment of a long-standing pledge. U2 had been asked to perform there during the Zoo TV Tour and all four had been eager to oblige. But other parties, having investigated the feasibility of such an event, had been forced to conclude that it would not have been possible at that time. It was explained to Bono that people standing in queues to get into the gig could literally have come under sniper fire.

The situation was markedly different now; indeed, the authorities were keen to make a fuss of the world-famous rock band that wanted to perform in their country. After touchdown at the airport, U2 were swept by an impressive police escort to meet Alija Izetbegovic, the President of Bosnia and Herzegovina. Bono gave the President a first edition book of poems by W. B. Yeats and talked to him about his country's problems.

To Bono, having seen for himself the destruction that war had wrought on Sarajevo, it verged upon the surreal that the people should want the flashy razzmatazz of a rock gig. The band had been fearful of in any way appearing to represent anything facile or patronizing. But it was pretty much impressed on them that the citizens not only wanted them there, they were also looking for the works – 35-foot lemon and all. It seemed that part of the reason why they were so insistent on this was because for a brief moment in time it signalled a return to normality.

The stadium, which had had to be rebuilt in the years since Sarajevo had hosted the glittering, globally watched 1984 Winter Olympics, prepared then to accommodate the Pop Mart show in all its bright glory. The support for the night was made up of local bands, including two rock acts Sikter and Protest and a choir, and the atmosphere was building to fever pitch.

This gig has to rank as one of U2's most unique appearances. A sizeable chunk of the audience was composed of uniformed soldiers from the peacekeeping forces that were present in the region (indeed, members of the Nato-led troops had swept the venue in advance, for bombs). Special trains had been laid on to ferry fans from across the country and from other former Yugoslav republics, bringing together for an evening people from the bitterly divided country.

Tickets had been made available through an international civilian organization specifically in place to work at strengthening the peace. U2 gig posters were pasted willy-nilly on top of weathered pictures of the Bosnian Serb leader Radovan Karadzic, now indicted as a war criminal. And the money generated by this gig would be donated to the hospital rebuilding programme in Sarajevo.

It was an emotional experience for Bono. Earlier in the day he had been greatly moved when a couple of small local children had solemnly handed him a few spent bullets which had been dug out of their bedroom wall at home. In their innocence, they had bizarrely gift-wrapped them as a present for him.

With the best will in the world, though, the gig, before roughly 45,000, did not go smoothly because fairly early on Bono lost his voice. On and off throughout the tour he had been plagued with this problem – a frontman's occupational hazard, made worse by his being a smoker.

He was gutted, though, that it should strike on that particular night. As it happened, the generosity and the huge reservoir of goodwill among the crowd was enough to buoy Bono up as the audience sang, hummed, even whistled as best they could, to help out.

Weeks earlier, Bono had anticipated that this gig would be the high spot of the whole trip for him. Soon after, he declared, 'It was one of the toughest and one of the sweetest nights of my life.'

Bono entered a reflective period immediately after Sarajevo. It was impossible to experience, even briefly, life in that region and to emerge unscathed. The harsh reality of what he had seen and heard concentrated his mind once more on what really mattered in life.

The European leg had ended in September. Despite what had been in some ways a less than smooth start, the Pop Mart tour was well on its way towards breaking records.

U2's sales statistics too were making interesting reading. Of the seventy-seven million album sales notched up worldwide, as at September 1997 thirty million of those had been bought in the USA. It was a warming thought, considering that in three weeks' time the North American second leg of Pop Mart was about to begin.

CHAPTER 12

Pacifist

B **Y THE TIME U2** took the show back to North America and
Canada, opening at the Skydome Stadium in Toronto on 26
October 1997, Pop Mart was being recognized and enjoyed
as a clever satire on consumer culture.

In Britain their latest single 'Please'/'Dirty Day', released three
weeks earlier, had racked up a number seven hit. The record's sleeve
showed four of the most prominent players in Irish politics – Sinn
Fein president Gerry Adams, Democratic Unionist Party leader the
Reverend Ian Paisley, John Hume leader of the Social Democratic
and Labour Party, and the leader of the Ulster Unionist Party David
Trimble.

In the coming months the band would dip its collective toe
further into the shark-infested waters of the political situation in
Ireland, but right then, as the four knuckled down to the business
of entertaining the masses, Adam Clayton had problems of his own.
The day after the tour recommenced, a 34-year-old local man was
reported to have been arrested in Toronto and charged with criminal harrassment.

He had allegedly been stalking the U2 bass player for three
years. He is also said to have relentlessly bombarded the band's

office in Dublin with telephone calls, calling upwards of 200 times a day. And the previous year, in March 1996, apparently the same man had flown to Dublin, whereupon he had been arrested very near Clayton's home.

The arrest in Toronto had occurred hours before the gig at the Skydome Stadium. The man appeared in court for a bail hearing on 28 October, when he was remanded in custody, the hearing resuming before a Justice of the Peace the next day.

Regardless of whether or not this man posed an actual threat to Adam Clayton's physical safety, his behaviour was an unnerving experience in an already celebrity-obsessed culture.

The line between reality and fantasy can get blurred for performers as well as fans. So, to avoid a repeat of the confusion that had, for some people, infiltrated the Zoo TV Tour, this time around the band decided it was essential to preserve their sanity in the midst of the cyclone of touring. And this they did by devoting as much free time as possible to the normal things in life. For instance, from the start of Pop Mart, they had made a point of having their family members and some friends come out to join them at regular intervals.

Ali Hewson had her own commitments and sometimes it was *her* turn to go abroad on business, particularly since she had become actively involved with the Chernobyl Children's Project. The CCP had been founded by Adi Roche and since Ali's first trip to Chernobyl in 1993, she had travelled to the Ukraine in western Russia a further seven times usually as part of a mission to bring aid and assistance to the chronically ill children, some 2,500 miles away in Belarus.

Bono and Ali arranged their travels to ensure that their own children always had at least one parent with them. During Bono's absence on tour, therefore, Ali looked after the children at home and so, when U2 hit Miami in mid-November, she was able to join Bono and bring their two daughters. Bono enjoyed being with his girls and if it sometimes entailed them having to forfeit school time, Ali undertook the task of tutoring them to ensure that they kept up with their studies.

It was important to Bono and to Ali that Jordan and Memphis Eve were allowed to share in some of the adventures that went with the territory of their father's glitzy profession. It also opened their minds to different countries and cultures.

Even when his family could not accompany him, Bono often spent his spare time whilst on tour visiting museums, galleries and restaurants. He also enjoyed shopping sprees. In fact, his adrenalin-driven personality meant that he was practically in perpetual motion.

Being a night owl, he invariably kept late hours, sometimes still drinking more than he conceded was good for him. Other times he would be forever on the telephone, making contact with home or furthering his involvement in an ever lengthening list of worthy, weighty causes.

And it was not only with his time that Bono was generous. Wherever he prowled, in whichever city around the world, he could rarely walk by a homeless person living rough on the streets without discreetly slipping them a wad of money. Startled recipients could suddenly find in their hands a roll of notes amounting to hundreds in their country's currency. That it was impossible to help everyone was obvious. But when this proved to be true of yet another of his friends, it was to hit Bono hard.

After the sudden death of Greg Carroll in 1986, Bono had gone through a long phase when he had to stop his heart from lurching whenever the telephone rang, fearing that it heralded more bad news. Now, having just played a gig in New Orleans, U2 was en route to their next pit stop when Bono picked up the phone to discover that Michael Hutchence, frontman of the Australian rock band INXS, was dead.

On Saturday, 22 November 1997, the latest rock 'n' roll casualty had made international television news headlines – perhaps unsurprisingly, in view of the gruesome circumstances in which the tragedy had occurred.

Michael Hutchence had been found naked, hanged behind the door of a Sydney hotel room. Sordid speculation immediately ran wild as to whether the 35-year-old rock singer had died accidentally, having indulged in a lone bizarre sex game that had gone wrong, or intentionally, as a result of suicide.

INXS, and Michael Hutchence, had first come to prominence in the late 1980s, before going on to fill stadiums around the world, attracting legions of devoted fans. Fame and his dark-haired good looks had made Hutchence a natural magnet for a bevvy of beautiful women. But it was his high-profile involvement with the flamboyant English television presenter Paula Yates (then the wife of Boomtown Rats' vocalist Bob Geldof, and the mother of Geldof's three daughters) that had caught the attention of the British press from 1995 onwards.

Paula Yates had subsequently left Bob Geldof to be with Michael Hutchence and together they had had a daughter named Heavenly Hiraani Tiger Lily. In 1997, however, difficulties had arisen between Yates and her former husband, centring on the custody of the children of their marriage. And, whether or not it was true, in the immediate aftermath of Michael Hutchence's death, some newspaper reports suggested that distress over these difficulties had partly contributed to the Australian singer's depressed state of mind.

So many challenging and colourful theories erupted about the reasons behind his death that it was impossible – if it *was* suicide – for anyone to know why the young man had killed himself and in such a fashion. Bono, swamped by his immense shock and sense of loss, was unable to make *any* sense of his friend's death at all.

Bono had had Hutch (as his friends knew him) for a near neighbour for a period of time, during which he had got to know his fellow frontman as someone who was considerably more laid back than he himself was. Indeed, it was partly due to their many differences in personality, Bono believed, that they complemented each other so well as mates.

Certainly, their friendship had extended to discussing profound

above: For a man who is practically in perpetual motion, relaxation is important and Bono can party with the best of them.

Bono was honoured with a private audience with Pope John Paul II in Rome on 23 September 1999, during which His Holiness tried on Bono's 'Fly' dark glasses. Sadly for posterity, the Vatican destroyed the photograph that was taken of the Pontiff in funky mood.

above: Up close and personal. Communication with the audience has always been an integral part of Bono's passionate live performances.

opposite: Bono and Alison Stewart met while still at school. They married in 1982 and had their fourth child in May 2001. Rarely photographed together, Ali guards their privacy and always prefers to carve her own independent career path.

left: Bono with UN Secretary General Kofi Annan. Bono's crusading zeal in support of efforts to cancel Third World debt has earned the singer deep respect from many of the world's leading political and religious figures.

below: At the 43rd Grammy Awards show at the Staples Center, Los Angeles, February 2001, U2 took three awards on the night. Backstage, referring to their triple win, Bono confessed, 'I don't remember really wanting it the way we wanted it tonight'.

and personal questions of life and death. Bono was even more baffled by his friend's death because the act of committing suicide had cropped up during one particular, and fairly recent, conversation. And Bono clearly recalled that Hutch had echoed his own conclusion that suicide was a stupid, not to mention a selfish, act; Bono did not know Michael Hutchence to be a selfish man.

Paramount then, over and above the usual feeling of inadequacy that he should have somehow been able to anticipate his friend's hour of need, there was a deep confusion in his mind. Bono could not figure out what had happened that night in the Sydney hotel room; he had a hard enough time working out how he felt about it.

Inescapably, Michael Hutchence's shocking death weighed heavily on the singer in the closing stages of this leg of the tour, but it did so without impinging on his performance onstage. Meanwhile, Bono's off-stage state of mind was also being affected by a touch of touring fatigue.

Like the others, he had been living out of a suitcase for months now. And by the time U2 arrived on 2 December at the Autodrome in Mexico City, Bono was at the point of waking up only to wonder which city he was in.

Perhaps it was a combination of fatigue and the effects of performing in a high-altitude atmosphere, but the first night in Mexico City, before a host of local dignitaries and celebrities, as well as fans, was not a success. Not mincing his words, Bono called it 'crap' and a 'let down'. But the band redeemed themselves the following evening, and this second Mexico City gig was filmed.

Exactly ten days later, the North American and Canadian leg of the tour ended at the Kingdome Stadium in Seattle. Just over a week after that, the second UK single of the year, 'If God Will Send His Angels'/'Mofo', emerged on 20 December, to drop anchor at number twelve. By this time Bono was in Mostar in Bosnia to take part in the opening ceremony of a new music therapy centre by the War Child charity.

The initial parameters of any U2 tour are prone to expand. Four days before the end of January 1998, the band proved that they had a way to go yet, as Pop Mart pushed into the South American continent to play a series of dates that began at the Nelson Piquet Autodrome Internacional in Rio de Janeiro, Brazil. By early February, the list would also embrace a three night sell-out stint at the River Plate Stadium in Buenos Aires in Argentina.

After the sobering recent events, the frontman seemed to be retrieving some of his usual sense of fun. When U2 won the Brit Award for Best International Group, on 9 February, Bono delivered his acceptance speech – beamed by satellite to the ceremony in London – from inside the mirrorball lemon stage prop.

His more relaxed attitude was also obvious during a more intimate engagement than normal before an audience of less than 14,000 people at the Burswood Dome in Perth, on 17 February, which opened U2's brief foray into Australia and New Zealand.

A visit to Japan featured next, before U2 made their debut performance in South Africa on 16 March, appearing at the Green Point Stadium in Cape Town. Five days later, this final leg of the tour ended with a gig at the Athletic Park in Johannesburg. Bono had been thrilled to be breaking new ground.

He had also had a long-standing ambition to meet President Nelson Mandela and he was hoping to fulfil this dream before leaving the country.

Throughout Nelson Mandela's twenty-eight years of imprisonment, he had been a global symbol of the fight against apartheid. Following his eventual release from jail in 1990 (an event that was televized live around the world), amid great political change, Mandela crowned the establishment of a new apartheid-free order in South Africa by rising to become the country's first democratic President. Just prior to the Athletic Park gig it had looked promising that President Mandela might manage to find an opening in his busy schedule to meet the band. But, sadly, he was involved in a long-running court case and couldn't find the time.

Bono's admiration of Nelson Mandela had been coupled to his support of many others who had campaigned to end the oppression of black South Africans – organizations such as Amnesty International and individuals, notable among whom is Archbishop Desmond Tutu, a Nobel Peace Prize winner. By 1998 the Archbishop was Chairman of the Truth and Reconciliation Committee which had been set up in South Africa.

Whilst in Cape Town, U2 was honoured to meet with Desmond Tutu who, in turn, holds the band in great esteem. The Archbishop says:

> They visited us here in South Africa when they came to the Truth and Reconciliation Commission and everybody was just bowled over with them.
>
> One has been very, very impressed with their social consciousness. They were very strongly aware of the anti-apartheid struggles, which they supported and this is something that thrilled us. When they came to the Commission they were all great fun. I think that they are tremendous young people. They are young people with very considerable idealism. And with Bono, it obviously shines through. Especially, when he has taken off his dark glasses!

On 21 March 1998 the eleven-month long Pop Mart world tour finally wrapped. During this mammoth excursion, U2 had played to close on four million people, grossing several million pounds to add to their overflowing coffers. Like their Zoo TV outing, Pop Mart had once more redefined stadium entertaining as the rock scene knew it.

Despite the various slings and arrows suffered along the way, the overall verdict was that U2 had, via its projection of artifice, in a back-to-front way, succeeded in reclaiming its sincerity.

Naturally the band had their critics, who continued to believe that U2 had strayed away into strange territory. Bono acknowledged this fact. But neither he, nor the rest of the band, was prepared to let the fear of upsetting critics ever stop them experimenting. Bono stated that, artistically speaking, 'You must not find yourself tiptoe-ing.'

So, Pop Mart had pleased the eye and stimulated the senses, while at the same time slipping in a few deeply meaningful songs.

And it had been another rollercoaster experience. For any major touring band, metaphorically living in each other's pockets, the long spells spent together often lead to tension, tiredness and claustro-phobia, even in-fighting. Yet, U2 continued to escape this fate and they returned to Ireland at the end of March as close friends as ever.

Few major rock bands of long standing manage to avoid the revolving door when it comes to personnel. U2's enviable secret was thought to be a combination of factors, one of which was the stabi-lizing effect of having a constant management and support network of staff around them. Many people in key positions in the full-time organization are familiar faces stretching back over most of the band's twenty-odd years as recording artistes.

Undoubtedly, though, the main reason was that, because they had formed a band as very young teenagers, they had grown up in life and in the music business together. They were also free of the ruinous jealousies over women and the endless jockeying for prominence that frequently causes schisms in otherwise successful bands.

The dedication of all four to the band had never wavered and the fact that they all lived in Dublin – within a few minutes driving distance of each other – also helped. And to those who encountered U2 at rest whilst on the road it was remarkably refreshing not to experience the odious exhibition of overblown ego or even the lack of basic manners that tended to mar the behaviour of some super-stars.

In Bono's case, his personality had barely altered. Still the eternal talker, he could be passionately intense on a serious topic, and the next moment, equally entertaining on a lighter subject. He enjoys a good debate about books or relating the experiences he has notched up on the band's foreign travels. Religion and art can usually be guaranteed to get him going. Yet, when the tables are turned, the ultra-talkative Bono is also an intent listener.

Once home in Ireland, it was his voice that became Bono's immediate concern. To some extent, he had been prepared to accept that his vocal cords would act up now and then during nightly gigs on the road. But the severe difficulties that he had endured during the latest tour were unacceptable. As U2 prepared to rest up for a while, he consulted hospital specialists about the condition.

Whilst a variety of exploratory tests were carried out on his throat, Bond reluctantly began to contemplate the awful prospect that he might be forced to give up his singing career altogether. However, these dark anxieties were soon laid to rest when it was discovered that the main root cause boiled down to allergies. Dietary changes and reducing his alcohol consumption were recommended, as was quitting smoking.

While Bono had been concerned about the state, and future, of his vocal cords, another kind of voice was being heard. On 10 April 1998, after what seemed an eternity of delicate and difficult negotiation, a historic political agreement had been brokered at Stormont Castle by former American Senator George Mitchell, the British Prime Minister Tony Blair and the Irish Prime Minister Bertie Ahern with eight political parties in Northern Ireland.

The Good Friday Agreement, as it was called, was intended to unite the differing political opinions and to channel all towards the common goal of bringing about a lasting peace. It aimed to put a stop to sectarian and political violence and pave the way for the establishment of a power-sharing executive – unionists and nationalists sitting together in cabinet.

There was to be a joint referendum in Northern Ireland and in the Irish Republic on whether or not to implement the terms of this momentous accord in just over a month's time, and so began a 'Yes' and a 'No' campaign to try to persuade all Irish citizens over the age of eighteen.

The 'Yes' campaign had the high-profile support of Presidents Bill Clinton and Nelson Mandela. Ulster Unionist Party leader David Trimble also endorsed the 'Yes' vote, as did the SDLP leader John Hume. Bono plainly revealed his admiration for the veteran civil rights campaigner, and friend, when he described John Hume as a real hero; indeed he even went so far as to dub him the present-day Martin Luther King.

As the weeks went by, opinion polls began to suggest that support to implement the peace accord might be faltering. With just days to go before Friday, 22 May, the 'Yes' campaign needed to pull something out of the hat. Time was drastically short, but then one of the campaign workers based at the SDLP's headquarters in Belfast, Tim Attwood, suddenly hit on the idea of organizing a free concert for peace.

To help to mobilize the large youth vote, Tim Attwood knew that it ought to be a rock gig. He was aware of the long-standing friendship between John Hume and Bono and he used this connection to put the prospect of headlining at such an event to U2. Despite the extreme short notice, the band responded that it was a great idea and so the gig was immediately announced. The date was fixed for the next day, Tuesday 19 May, and it was to be staged at Belfast's Waterfront Hall.

Behind this announcement, there had been a frantic flurry of activity. U2's promised participation brought a flood of media interest in the event, with live broadcasts being hastily arranged. And the idea had also sprouted, during one of the many meetings held at campaign headquarters, that John Hume and David Trimble should be seen together at this gig.

The 2,000-seater Waterfront Hall, sited on the banks of the River Lagan, was an apt venue. Having been built in the wake of an IRA and loyalist ceasefire four years earlier, and with its facilities being shared by both communities, it had come to symbolize the regeneration that would be possible in a peaceful, modern and forward-looking Northern Ireland.

All four U2 members converged on Belfast from different parts of the world for the event. Bono, accompanied by Edge, arrived at the venue ahead of Larry Mullen and Adam Clayton, to be welcomed by Ash, another band that would be performing that night. The addition of the younger rock band from Downpatrick in Northern Ireland meant that, between them, U2 and Ash, represented, musically, two generations from either side of the Irish border.

Ash's lead singer Tim Wheeler joined Bono and Edge, along with John Hume and David Trimble, at an impromptu press conference held in the early evening just before the gig. Speaking for U2, Bono expressed their delight at having been invited to join the two politicians who were among those who had given so much to get Ireland this far.

Bono passionately urged those who remained sceptical to take that leap of faith and still vote 'Yes', not to risk squandering this historic chance to reshape Ireland's future.

The backdrop to the stage inside the hall read 'YES – Make Your Own History'. In addition to politicians and journalists, the crowd mainly comprised teenagers from Catholic and Protestant schools. Ash took to the stage first for this televized event. Then Bono and Edge joined them to perform the Beatles' number 'Don't Let Me Down'.

U2 subsequently took over and found a wildly appreciative audience. Their set included such numbers as the Ben E. King classic 'Stand By Me', John Lennon's peace anthem 'Give Peace A Chance' and U2's own 'One'.

But the most enduring image of the gig came when Bono asked David Trimble and John Hume up on stage in what would be the veteran politicians' first joint appearance of the referendum campaign. Bono introduced them as two of the architects of the peace agreement, two men willing to leave the past behind in order to forge ahead.

Standing between the pair, Bono, the son of a mixed marriage, physically and symbolically bridging the sectarian divisions, simultaneously raised aloft David Trimble's left arm and John Hume's right arm in a salute. And a great cheer rang out.

The sight struck a definite chord with many people, including Ireland's former Taoiseach, Garret Fitzgerald who recalls, 'When Bono brought John Hume and David Trimble together it was very striking. That was a very dramatic moment. But Bono has that strong commitment to issues in Northern Ireland and to other issues more globally. And he has used his considerable influence, derived from his popularity, very constructively.'

Bono then led the assembled gathering in a moving tribute to the 3,000 victims of the nearly three decades of bloodshed, so far, in Northern Ireland, and followed this by calling for a one-minute silence. Bono brought the silence to an end with the words, 'Thanks for your patience. Bless you.'

The result of the referendum was that the 'Yes' vote carried the day – by a resounding 71 per cent in Northern Ireland and a whopping 95 per cent in the Irish Republic. Three years later, the relevant parties were still trying to make it work. But the peace gig came to be seen as one of the critical moves made in the closing stages of electioneering, and U2 had been proud to play a small, but vital, part in the process.

For the remainder of the summer, Bono kept a low profile, giving himself the chance to fully recuperate from the tour and to nurse his voice into better health. The only other campaign he involved himself in was signing a petition in mid-October, raised by Amnesty International in support of the fiftieth anniversary of the Universal Declaration of Human Rights.

On the last day of October, U2's only single of the year was released. 'Sweetest Thing'/'Stories for Boys (Live 1981)' fizzled out at an unimpressive number sixty-three in America, but bristled in Britain at number three.

The previous month the band had negotiated an extra recording deal with Polygram that was unusual in the sense that it involved no new material being recorded. Instead it was for three compilation albums.

The first of this trilogy was released on 14 November 1998 titled *The Best of 1980–1990/The B-Sides*. It was a limited edition double CD, with the second disc containing the B sides of singles for the same period. It topped the British album charts and stopped just one place shy of that in America.

A second version of this first of three compilation albums, this time titled only *The Best of 1980–1990* (i.e. minus the disc containing B sides), was released two weeks later. Such was the devotion of the British U2 fans that it also fared well, reaching number four. In America there was less enthusiasm for this extra version and it pulled up at number forty-five.

Having lain low for half of 1998, U2 returned to the public eye on 20 November when they took part in a special edition of RTE's Friday night live talk show, called *The Late Late Show*, hosted by Gay Byrne.

Earlier in the year, on Saturday, 15 August, in the teeth of the peace efforts, a terrorist car bomb (thought to be the work of a splinter group) had exploded in the heart of the busy town centre of Omagh in Northern Ireland, killing twenty-eight people, injuring hundreds, and maiming some for life.

This special two and a half hour edition of *The Late Late Show* was intended as a tribute to the victims of this atrocity and also as a fund-raising event; some relatives of the dead and injured were present in the television audience. Other guest performers included the Corrs and Bob Geldof. U2 performed 'North and South of the River' and 'All I Want is You', after which Gay Byrne interviewed Bono.

At the close of 1998, aged thirty-eight, Bono now conceded that he had grown more at ease with his role of rock star. He had found, he said, a way of playing with it. Yet, at the same time, he remained deadly serious about the music. He would talk about the need for U2 to preserve their 'emotional terrain'. And in the year ahead he saw them concentrating on appreciating and developing the band's uniqueness.

As had been witnessed this past twelve months, however, Bono's identification with political and social causes had also strengthened – a characteristic that would show no signs of abating as the decade entered its final year.

CHAPTER 13

Crusader

B Y 1999 THE NUMBER of social and political causes on behalf of which Bono could be relied upon to passionately petition was already more than any working rock superstar could reasonably be expected to actively involve himself with.

However, in the final twelve months of the decade, leading up to the historic dawn of a new Millennium, Bono would become a vociferous spokesman for Jubilee 2000, an organization whose aim is to eradicate world poverty by persuading rich industrialized nations to write off the vast outstanding debts owed to them by Third World countries.

Because of his renowned social activism, the singer receives many requests from charities seeking his high-profile support – too many calls to answer. But Bono had been motivated to add Jubilee 2000 to his workload because he believed that the organization's strategy, while ambitious, had a positive chance of producing real results, of making a tangible change for the better (in contrast to some other, perhaps well-meaning but ultimately ineffectual campaigns).

His initial introduction to Jubilee 2000 had come via the organization's partner for strategy and global initiatives, Jamie Drummond. Says Jamie:

Back in 1995 it was the tenth anniversary of Live Aid and I worked at that time taking film crews around the north of Ethiopia to the areas most hit by the famine. While there I observed that yes, okay, the money from Live Aid had certainly gone towards saving lives. But I also observed that Ethiopia was scheduled to make debt payments in 1995, 1996 and 1997 of an average of $500 million a year, i.e. something like two and a half times the money that had been raised by Live Aid.

Live Aid had been a moment of idealism and optimism and a lot of young people had got very excited and involved in something that didn't seem to be about their immediate interests, and this in the greedy 1980s. It had been one of those special moments, especially in the media. A lot of people had been inspired by what Bob Geldof, supported by people like Bono, did in Live Aid and Band Aid. So a kind of seedling was there.

It just seemed like an obvious point to think what a shame one couldn't persuade the same forces that had been behind Live Aid to do something that, this time, wouldn't be just throwing money at a problem, not that Live Aid can be described just as that. But maybe people should be trying to go to the underlying structural causes of poverty, rather than just dealing with the symptoms of it.

In 1995 only about half a dozen people had ever heard of Jubilee 2000. Then the next year their offices turned up next to my office at Christian Aid. The director was Ann Pettifor and she had an assistant and I put it to the two of them that I was going to try and basically persuade the music industry to support this young campaign. And, of course, one of the first people that came to mind was Bono – he having played a big role in Live Aid, but also since then having gone on from strength to strength. He also had a track record of having worked on issues like apartheid. He had worked with

Amnesty International on human rights matters and had worked with Greenpeace.

Plus, in Bono's case he has some kind of ability to communicate and he possesses a religious, or rather, spiritual conviction in what he is doing. Jubilee 2000 does not have to appeal to one on the basis of its spiritual inspiration. It appeals to very hard-headed people, economists and politicians. But I knew that Bono would find that extremely appealing.

So the campaigning skills of the aid agencies became combined with the urgency and inspiration of Christians who believed that the Millennium was a special time. The Millennium too was the moment we were all focused on and this helped to generate the sense of 'We gotta do this now!' This was a one-off extraordinary time. In a sense that was just a great marketing idea that happens to have been in the Bible.

I wanted to put it to Bono but U2 were on their Pop Mart Tour in 1997 and it wasn't a good time to get through to him. I pursued a number of other avenues and in due course Mohammed Ali agreed to be our international ambassador. The Dalai Lama, David Bowie, Sir Anthony Hopkins – a whole host of people – started to come on board and the Jubilee 2000 petition started to grow.

Jamie Drummond, however, continued to pursue Bono's involvement, which eventually came about through a number of connections in and around Island Records. Jamie continues:

Richard Constant is a remarkable and unsung character. He is the chief lawyer for the Universal Music Group and he, along with a couple of others, were persuaded to put the campaign firmly in front of Bono and to encourage him to support it.

It was in 1998 that Bono first called. At that time there was the south-east Asian financial crisis happening and basically the first time I heard from Bono, down the phone he said, 'Hi. It's Bono. This situation in south-east Asia? Wouldn't that mean that your campaign is not going to get anywhere, because everyone is going to be frightened of world recession?' I had to guess whether this was someone downstairs trying to pull my leg, or whether it was really Bono calling me up and throwing this very difficult question straight off at me. But it was him.

His involvement was going to take various different guises, but we started out having a series of meetings in Dublin at Principle Management offices, which really took off at the end of 1998 and the beginning of 1999. Bono invited to these meetings people like the promoter Harvey Goldsmith and Bob Geldof, wanting their experience and their wisdom on how to make this a music industry inspired campaign.

As the strategy that was thrashed out was then put into practice, Bono would begin to devote a substantial amount of time to the organization.

Jamie Drummond explains:

The first thing that Bono really did, apart from doing bits of petition signing, was in mid-February 1999 he came along to the Brit Awards ceremony in London and at that ceremony he made a speech calling upon politicians to cancel the debt. It wasn't scripted into the show. It was a surprise event.

Bono was then given the Freddie Mercury Award for good causes and he duly went down into the crowd and handed the award straight on to Mohammed Ali. If you like, that was a golden moment because it launched the campaign in the tabloid newspapers in a way that we had not managed to do before.

We had managed to get some head of steam in the *Financial Times*, but not a lot. And the *Guardian* loved the campaign. But it was really the celebrity thing around the Brit Awards that February which forced politicians to realize that they could not afford to ignore the post bag that was swelling with letters from people from all walks of life in the UK who were calling on Prime Minister Tony Blair and the Chancellor Gordon Brown to do more. And, within a couple of days of the Brit Awards, Gordon Brown made a statement about cancelling an extra £50 million at the forthcoming G8 summit.

The following month Bono began writing a series of open letters to major newspapers around the world, to focus publicity on the issue of dropping the debt. In June the leading industrialized countries gathered for the G8 summit in Cologne in Germany, with government leaders in attendance, and Jubilee 2000 planned to take full advantage of the event.

A protest concert, hopefully featuring top acts, was mooted for Cologne to coincide with this international political gathering. And in his letters to newspapers Bono was able to confirm that there was a great deal of support among his peers for the campaign. Heavy hitters in the music world were showing willing, at least in principle, to the idea of participating in a gig. And before long this proposed single gig folded out into a potential series of performances.

Whether or not such a thing would be feasible remained to be seen, but Bono did commit himself from the outset to taking part in a human chain which, it was hoped, would stretch all the way around the building in which the world leaders would be gathered. The sight of Bono back on his soap box drew some fire from the media at first, but he remained undeterred.

Neither he, nor U2, were slow either to do what they could for the victims of the latest humanitarian catastrophe to hit the news headlines. At the end of March 1999 a major military offensive was underway in the Balkans to try to reverse President Slobodan Milosevic's Serbian army aggression against the people of Kosovo.

As so-called ethnic cleansing atrocities were carried out, a mass exodus of refugees poured, or were pushed, across borders into neighbouring countries. This endless flow of exhausted, starving and frightened hordes, with horrific stories to tell, ended up sheltering in massive tent cities of almost Biblical proportions, while the Nato alliance brought its firepower down on Belgrade in an attempt to bomb Milosevic into submission.

As international aid agencies struggled to cope with the ever-expanding tide of human misery, U2 were one of the first bands to announce that they stood ready to be involved in any fundraising music initiative that might be organized to help the displaced people.

With this intense preoccupation with the plight of the world's poor and needy, it was essential to find some light relief. Having been in New York City in January, Bono had returned to America at the beginning of March to be reunited with his friend Bob Dylan on stage at the opening night of the Mandalay Bay Hotel in Las Vegas. The sold-out show was at the hotel's House of Blues venue and Bono joined Dylan for the encore to the eighty-minute set, singing 'Knockin' On Heaven's Door' – U2's frontman once more at times ad-libbing his way through the lyrics.

Mid-month Bono then went back to New York to induct another of his heroes, Bruce Springsteen, into the Rock and Roll Hall of Fame. And by early April he finally wound his way back home to Ireland, to his children and to Ali who was once again pregnant – the baby being due in August.

It might have been easy, amid all the various irons on the fire, to forget that he had a day job. The Pop Mart Tour had ended over a year ago and the band had fairly quickly thereafter turned their thoughts to their next studio album, but had made little progress. They had plans to knuckle down again with producers Brian Eno and Daniel Lanois in late April, but before that Bono had time to indulge his continuing interest in film.

This month indeed marked the moment that Bono made his screen debut when he appeared as himself in *Entropy*, directed by Phil Joanou. The director, with whom U2 had worked on the *Rattle and Hum* rockumentary, had filmed an account of his own life story. And the modestly budgeted US$3 million independent movie, starring *Backbeat* star Stephen Dorff, premiered at the Los Angeles Independent Film Festival's opening night gala on 17 April 1999.

The plot, part of which involved a film-maker making a documentary about U2, had necessitated showing footage of a live U2 performance and Phil Joanou had joined the Pop Mart Tour in its final stages in South Africa for this purpose. Bono's was a very small appearance, but he had been happy to accommodate a friend. Joanou revealed that Bono had been his first port of call with his unusual script, because he knew the singer would encourage him to pursue his perhaps radical, certainly experimental, ideas to the full.

Bono's interest in film ensured that he was also in attendance in April when the Italian-American film director Martin Scorsese (whose credits include *Raging Bull*, *GoodFellas* and *The Age of Innocence*) held a master class on film directing at Ireland's only film studio, Ardmore Studios, on the outskirts of Dublin. Accompanied by U2's manager Paul McGuinness, Bono sat listening intently in the front row of the 300-strong audience.

As Scorsese later travelled on to the Cannes Film Festival, Bono turned his thoughts back to music and rejoined U2 in the studio. One of the tracks that would ultimately emerge from these protracted recording sessions would be a song called 'The Ground Beneath Her Feet'. This song, co-written by Bono and Salman Rushdie, and based on the writer's new novel of the same name, was a sad Celtic ballad and would eventually feature in the sound-track for *The Million Dollar Hotel*.

The new recording sessions hadn't progressed far when it became clear that they were going to be subject to several interruptions as a result of Bono's commitment to Jubilee 2000. Despite holding meetings in May with organization officials and others, it was proving difficult to put into practice the idea of mounting one or more concerts in Cologne. But one gig would ultimately be on the agenda, to be called 'Net Aid'.

Meanwhile, the idea of the peaceful demonstration in Cologne, in just over a month's time, was gathering pace. By now, Bono was in talks with fellow vocalist Perry Farrell, former frontman with the American hard rock band Jane's Addiction, to see if they could use their joint clout to recruit other high-profile music stars to the cause.

This consuming involvement ate into recording time, with the knock-on effect of considerably delaying progress on U2's album. But Bono knew that the others also supported the aims of Jubilee 2000. It was just as well, because the singer left his recording work behind again to head out to Cologne for the three-day G8 summit which commenced on Friday, 18 June.

The much-publicized human chain was originally supposed to involve as many as 70,000 volunteers. On the actual day that number, in reality, had shrunk to 20,000, but it was still a sizeable public show of strength. Bono joined in with the crowd in holding hands around the building wherein the world leaders were meeting. The main crux of their protest was that the current G8 proposals to help the world's poor nations were welcome but they did not go far enough.

As the most prominent figure in this delegation, Bono was acutely aware of the apparent absurdity of a well-heeled rock star becoming one of the main figureheads of a campaign against grinding poverty. However, celebrity involvement seemed to be the key to igniting the public pressure needed to influence the world's political leaders.

Bono, therefore, presented a debt relief petition to the G8 summit host, Germany's Chancellor Gerhard Schröder. And later, accompanied by Bob Geldof, Bono also talked about the campaign with Prime Minister Tony Blair. Edge, too, had taken time out from working on the album to be in Cologne for the peaceful protest but now both he and Bono returned to work.

Yet, within a fortnight, Larry Mullen, Adam Clayton and Edge were left to carry on without their singer again. This time Bono was off to America for a two-day session in a New Jersey basement recording studio commencing on 4 July.

He was going to work with the 27-year-old Haitian-born rapper Wyclef Jean, singer with the 1990s group The Fugees, on a charity single destined to become the official anthem of Net Aid. It was the first time Bono had worked with the hip hop artiste, though Wyclef Jean had admired the U2 singer for many years.

Following a couple of name changes, they eventually called the song which they co-wrote 'New Day'. Half the proceeds would go to Net Aid, and the other half would be donated to the Wyclef Jean Foundation which aided refugees.

A frequent visitor to the United States, Bono would return there in September. But in the meantime he arrived back in Ireland as it became clear that, unsurprisingly, the original autumn deadline for completion of the band's new album could not be met.

Bono also needed to keep his restless feet in Dublin at this point for an extra special reason as Ali's pregnancy entered its final days. She went into labour with their third child as the couple approached their seventeenth wedding anniversary in August. They named their first son Elijah Bob Patricius Guggi Q Hewson.

Far from mellowing the thirty-nine-year-old father of three, the new arrival made Bono see mankind's responsibilities to the planet and to the future of the human race in even starker relief. As Elijah was born into certain security, men, women and children at the end of the twentieth century were dying in their droves of starvation and of curable diseases. This bleak contrast added an extra fuel injection to an already bright flame, and before Elijah was one month old his father was back in America for an important four weeks' work on behalf of the world's poor.

On 8 September Bono teamed up with Wyclef Jean to perform their song 'New Day' at the United Nations amid much publicity. Then the pair gave a second performance of the number at a benefit gig on behalf of the Wyclef Jean Foundation, held at the Copacabana in New York City, and the single was released on 14 September.

Net Aid was an event set up by the United Nations, in association with Cisco Systems, as an anti-poverty initiative and the Internet would be used to promote it globally. A press conference to launch the Net Aid website was held in New York City's Millennium Hotel on the afternoon of 9 September, at which Bono was one of the guest speakers, along with the United Nations Secretary General Kofi Annan, David Bowie, Wyclef Jean and Sean Combs (better known as Puff Daddy).

The first people to officially click on to the website were President Bill Clinton, Prime Minister Tony Blair and ex-President Nelson Mandela and it was announced that three benefit gigs were to be simultaneously staged around the world on 9 October.

The gigs would be broadcast on the satellite music channels VH1 and MTV, as well as on the Net Aid website. The American gig would take place at the Giants Stadium in East Rutherford, New Jersey. This was where Bono intended to perform; and at the press conference it was announced that his fellow performers that day would feature Bon Jovi, Sting, Jimmy Page, Wyclef Jean and Zucchero.

London's concert was planned for the Wembley Arena and the line-up included David Bowie, Bryan Adams, Robbie Williams and George Michael. The third gig was to be an invitation-only show staged at the Palais des Nations in Geneva featuring Bryan Ferry, Des'ree, Michael Kamen and his orchestra, and Texas.

At the press conference the video of 'New Day' was premiered as Net Aid's anthem. Bono also took the opportunity to explain that, as U2 could not play at the Giants Stadium due to some family commitments of Edge's, that he and Wyclef Jean would be duetting instead.

With Net Aid one month distant, Bono pressed on with the business of taking Jubilee 2000's message to the highest level, knowing that his celebrity status could open some doors that would otherwise have remained firmly shut. Less than a fortnight after his American trip, Bono arrived in Italy to spearhead probably one of the most important Jubilee 2000 delegations – to try to secure the influential support of the Vatican.

Bono's meeting with Pope John Paul II on 23 September 1999 took place at the Pope's summer residence in Rome and proved to be a most memorable occasion for the singer.

Bono had disapproved of the restraining grip inherent in much of the Catholic faith and he later admitted that, prior to this privileged audience, he had experienced mixed feelings. 'I don't think I could have done it ten years ago,' he said.

However, the Polish Pontiff's blend of charisma, spirituality and courage deeply moved Bono. The Pope does not enjoy good health and seeing the frail old man conquer his ills to meet the delegation, and sincerely involve himself with the campaign's aims, drew the singer's admiration.

Heavy issues were at stake but there was also a lighter side to proceedings. Jamie Drummond, who was part of the delegation, recalls, 'The Pope gave Bono some rosary beads, just as he had given to the rest of the VIP advocates of the campaign. And in turn, Bono gave the Pope a book of poetry by Seamus Heaney, the Irish Laureate, and at the same time he also handed over his wraparound shades. And the Pope put them on!'

The rock frontman had respectfully teased the holy man about his natural showmanship, but the Pope then startled Bono by suddenly donning the dark wraparound glasses. Jamie Drummond declares, 'That was a key moment. Sadly, however, for posterity, the Vatican, who tightly controlled the coverage of the event, seem to have since destroyed the photograph of the Pope actually wearing Bono's shades. Which is a great tragedy, and a disservice to humanity.'

At a press conference after the audience, Bono related this moment to the international press pack, jokingly dubbing the Holy Father, 'The first funky Pontiff'. In all, it was an experience that Bono will always remember.

Having helped to secure Vatican support for Jubilee 2000, Bono spent several hours that day talking politics and humanitarian issues with the world's media. He repeatedly stressed the enormity of the plight faced by the Third World countries and the obscenity that in this day and age over a billion people should still be struggling to exist or were dying needlessly. His generation, he maintained, now regonized that it was no longer sufficient to throw spare change at the problem.

Wound up after the day's events, by midnight Bono was consequently far from ready for sleep. Despite the fact that he had to catch an early morning flight from Rome to Washington next day, he headed out to a restaurant, followed by a nightclub, accompanied by a couple of minders and a few friends who had travelled to Italy with him.

Such tireless energy was essential in order to meet all his commitments. But not all of them were guaranteed to reap the fullest rewards.

The massive Internet charity event Net Aid came and went on 9 October 1999 with mixed results. Jamie Drummond is frank. 'Net Aid was not a great success,' he says. 'And Bono didn't play a lead role in it, although some people made out that he did. He just did it to try to promote debt cancellation in America and at a strategically very important moment for us.'

The Palais des Nations gig in Geneva had always been intended to be a more select show and London's Wembley Arena concert, on balance, did best, pulling a crowd of 60,000. The major Giants Stadium gig in East Rutherford, New Jersey, however, brought its disappointments, primarily because the attendance figures were far lower than expected – reaching nowhere near the stadium's 75,000 capacity.

The organizers, of course, immediately put a spin on this and insisted that the intimate gig had had its merits. But many of those who did attend were frustrated by the time it took to strip down and change the various sets between acts. That said, there *were* highlights – one of which was the all-star performance to open the show of Bono and Wyclef Jean's song, 'New Day'.

Once Bono returned to the studio to resume work on U2's new album, each new day just brought the old problem of being so far behind schedule. Although Mullen, Edge and Clayton approved of Bono's work for Jubilee 2000, an element of contention must have broken through at times about the delays that the singer's frequent absences were causing.

Certainly, their slow progress could not be blamed entirely on these absences, but the drummer later revealed that there had been some pretty tough, and downright dark, moments for them behind closed doors.

The tide would turn in the new year. But, before then, it was Bono's efforts outside music that would put him back into the spotlight. At the MTV Europe Music Awards, staged at Dublin's Point Theatre on 11 November, the singer was given the Free Your Mind Award to honour his work for peace, for helping the 'Yes' vote to succeed in Northern Ireland and for his crusading zeal on behalf of the world's poorest and most vulnerable people.

The award was handed over to Bono at the ceremony by Rolling Stone Mick Jagger who jokingly warned the U2 frontman that he was flirting dangerously with sainthood. Accepting the honour, an emotional Bono admitted that such praise was only likely to make him worse.

Bono's humanitarian work was now bringing him the warmest respect from some of the world's most influential figures. United Nations Secretary General Kofi Annan says:

I have great admiration for Bono, both personally, and for his dedication to campaigning to end the crushing burden of Third World debt.

Through his stature in the worlds of music and entertainment, Bono has educated and inspired thousands of individuals, especially young people, to become involved in this vital political issue. He is a genuine friend of the United Nations, and has made a real difference to the lives of the world's poor.

Meanwhile, Archbishop Desmond Tutu says of Bono and of the rest of U2:

It is so very typical of them that they should have this concern and, in a way, to try to put their money where their mouths are. I mean, they have a very high profile and therefore are a very significant support for a crucial campaign. And I am just thrilled and can't find the words to commend them warmly enough for their stand.

It is a wonderful thing, because they could so easily not care. They are very wealthy and their own country is not doing badly. There is no reason why they should be concerned so much about things happening several thousands of miles away. I am very deeply touched that Bono and the rest of the band should work for countries that are usually not at the centre of the world's agenda.

The Free Your Mind Award must rank among Bono's most treasured possessions and a sense of contentment would have been beneficial to carry back into the recording studio as December loomed. The task with the new album was not to be underestimated. Once again, U2 were seeking not so much to re-invent themselves as to go back to where it had all begun. Bono later stated, 'You have the right to begin again. It's a spiritual principle.'

This time around they wanted to shed all artifice, any suggestion of intended irony. And for Bono, more than two decades on, it was important not to become jaded about songwriting. The metamorphosis required to translate hours of mental effort into a compact song of less than a handful of minutes' duration, and for it then to have the power to make an impact, still gave him a rush.

In writing this new material Bono wanted to get back to basics in every sense, to produce lyrics that related to people in their everyday, ordinary lives. He declared, 'I was looking for intimacies. This was no time for smart arse.'

Just as things appeared to be settling into the groove suddenly a mini-crisis erupted when Bono's laptop computer containing lyrics for the album and other work was stolen from the Clarence Hotel sometime on the night of Monday, 6 December.

When it was not found quickly, on Thursday band manager Paul McGuinness issued a statement to the press reporting the missing laptop computer and offering a £2,000 reward for its return. The statement ended: 'To anyone else, it's just a personal computer and a few pieces of paper. To Bono, it's much more important.'

The following day a member of the public who had innocently purchased the laptop from a third party came forward with the computer. Bono's relief at its return was especially deep because, as he now revealed, he had not backed up on disc any of his work for the past five months. In addition to the reward that the young man was entitled to claim, Bono offered to buy the guy a new laptop.

While the recording studio sessions resumed, Bono continued to keep in touch with progress being made in the efforts to cancel the debt. So he was especially thrilled when, on 19 December, Chancellor Gordon Brown announced Britain's decision to cancel hundreds of millions of pounds of debt owed by Third World countries to the UK.

Bono told Sky TV news viewers, 'You can't over-emphasise what has happened here. It's a gigantic thing.' And he went on to loudly applaud Gordon Brown and Prime Minister Tony Blair.

By now, Bono was well accustomed to sudden switches of hat, from rock star to humanitarian, and when lobbying politicians he often rubbed shoulders with the world's leading figures. And so it came as no surprise when Bono, with Ali, featured among the invited guests at the Millennium Eve celebrations hosted by President Bill Clinton and First Lady Hillary Clinton on 31 December 1999.

The Hewsons were among 360 guests for the formal official dinner held at the White House earlier in the evening, before the focus shifted to a Millennium gala spectacular held at the Lincoln Memorial. Here, around 300,000 people congregated for the countdown to midnight.

There was also a gala concert at the Lincoln Memorial that showcased a variety of musical genres including gospel, opera, rap, jazz, folk and rock, in which Bono took part. Then, at the stroke of midnight, the year date 1999 being projected onto the side of the massive white obelisk, changed to 2000, exactly as fireworks exploded in a brilliant shower of sparks and shards of light above Washington DC.

The wave of optimism which washed in with the new century was reflected in an improvement in the atmosphere at the recording studio, and the band's better humour facilitated faster progress.

The thought had occurred to some that perhaps it wasn't that helpful for U2 to be recording in a studio in Dublin. For, while it was a definite plus to be able to return to their respective homes every day after work finished in the studio, it was also true that having to switch off from music and on to life's domestic problems could sometimes disturb continuity and affect progress.

Nevertheless, they now seemed to have found fresh impetus and sharper concentration, and Edge commented, 'We felt that the chemistry of the band was right.' They had retrieved, he felt, the excitement that is inherent in creating new music. Bono's voice too had acquired new textures, contributing further dimensions to the overall sound. The drummer remarked that it almost seemed as if Bono's voice had only now broken.

Bono's delight at the way things were going in the recording studio was enhanced by the long-awaited arrival of the movie *The Million Dollar Hotel*. The romantic thriller, which Bono tagged 'a dark fable about the redemptive power of love', premiered on 10 February 2000 at the 50th Berlin Film Festival. Bono, who makes a small cameo appearance in the film, was in Berlin for the event and he also attended the post-screening news conference alongside the film's director, Wim Wenders.

Having written the original story from which Nicholas Klein had adapted the screenplay, Bono attempted to shed some light on the film's plot and its very disparate characters. 'All cinema, all theatre is, to a degree, voyeurism,' he stated, but he also maintained that the film-makers had handled that particular aspect of the movie with some respect.

The Million Dollar Hotel was one of only three German films, among a total of twenty-one movies in competition at the festival, and it won the Silver Eagle award, although the art house movie would go on to receive mixed reviews. Ever the optimist, when tackled about the poorer reviews Bono suggested that perhaps those critics needed to see the movie more than once to grasp it.

Bono's travels in Europe did not end with this Berlin trip. On 23 February he was back in Rome. The Pope had declared the year 2000 to be a 'Holy Year' and on behalf of Jubilee 2000 Bono was still rapping on doors – this time that of Italian Prime Minister Massimo D'Alema, to persuade him to sanction the cancellation of more Third World debt.

Days later, accompanied by Edge, Bono appeared on stage at the finale of the week-long annual music festival held at the Italian Riviera resort of San Remo. Before the live audience and the millions watching on national television, he thanked the Pope and Prime Minister D'Alema for their support.

The intense commitment that Bono had given to help those fighting world poverty had not snuffed out his passion for fighting other battles. The band's pedigree here also stood up well and for this, as well as for their music, on 20 March Bono's home town honoured U2 with the Freedom of Dublin City, which was awarded to all four by Mayoress Mary Freehill.

Bono, Larry Mullen, Adam Clayton and Edge then signed Dublin's Roll of Honour – past recipients of the Freedom of Dublin City included Nelson Mandela and the assassinated American President John F. Kennedy.

While sensible of the honour bestowed upon them, the band found some amusement in the fact that the privileges allowed under this award included the right to graze sheep on the city's parks and to park a vehicle wherever one liked – the latter right being something, his bandmates chorused, that Bono already did anyway.

The subject of Bono and vehicles, in fact, was a somewhat sensitive one. Bono was such a shockingly bad driver that the cry invariably went up never to get into a car with the singer unless you had a particularly robust nervous system!

Back at the studio, an announcement had been made in the second week of March that U2's tenth studio album would finally be released in October 2000.

The band had given themselves until the end of August to complete the work. And with his new deadline to concentrate the mind, the final push involved putting in even longer hours at the studio, often eating dinner on the premises. A cook prepared the food on another level of the building and they could all eat together before returning immediately to work.

Anticipation – for this two-years-in-the-making album – began to grow from the date of that announcement. Like the rest of U2, Bono was setting a lot of store by this new material. He had no interest in sitting on his laurels and adamantly refused to accept that U2 had had their heyday. He had been part of this band from the age of sixteen. In May 2000 Bono had turned forty but he remained as keen as ever that U2 should become better with each decade.

The announcement of the forthcoming album was augmented by a pledge that U2 would be hitting the road again, although at this stage the tour details had yet to be finalized. Pop Mart may have ended in March 1998 and it had been almost two years since a U2 record release, yet press and media interest in them had never waned and the demand for interviews sprang up at once.

For the band the 1990s had been a decade of experimentation that had not always proved popular with their rank and file supporters. The forthcoming album promised to leave all that behind. Larry Mullen, for one, though, was not blasé about their prospects. He stated, 'I'm under no illusions about the difficulty of recapturing ground that we've lost.'

While there were still two months before the album's release, a steady stream of news leaked out about it and Bono's position quickly became clear. He enthused about the magical clarity of the music, and the lyrics reflecting what he called the 'pure joy' of being in a rock band. It was, he was prepared to pronounce in advance, going to be a very special album.

It had also been an exceptionally long time in coming, for which Bono had to take his share of responsibility. But it had been a hectic and special period – in the last twelve months alone his first son had been born and he had a major award to honour his efforts for peace and for a better world.

The new Millennium was a time to look forward, however, and he wanted to shrug off some of the signs that he was once more assuming the mantle of sainthood.

And the signs were there. One of the many publications to show an official photograph of Bono's audience with Pope John Paul II even carried the witty caption, 'His Holiness meets the Pope'. Having been afforded Messianic status in the 1980s, Bono was even less comfortable with the prospect of it now. He knew that he was, on the contrary, a peaceful man yes, but one within whom various forms of aggression still raged.

From time to time, Bono would publicly stress that that was why he admired true paragons of peace – people like Martin Luther King and Mahatma Gandhi – because he wished fervently that he could himself aspire to that level of pure Christianity.

Instead, he was all too aware that the rage that had burned inside him since his youth could still spill over. He appeared to be being somewhat harsh on himself, however, when he went so far as to say that he was capable of exhibiting a brutal kind of aggression. But, undoubtedly, he firmly believed that it was essential to acknowledge one's demons in order to control them.

Such candour might have been intended to stifle the perception of sainthood but it also illuminated the fact that Bono was someone who was as uncompromising with himself as with others. It made him frank, sometimes funny, maybe flawed, but never phoney.

CHAPTER 14

Ambassador

BEFORE LONG, BONO would become heavily immersed in band business. But, still, the imminent release of U2's new album and the preparation for their subsequent world tour did not prevent him from continuing to be involved with Jubilee 2000 work.

As the charity's lead spokesperson, he was already a man with a mission, who was, by design, hard to ignore. This was particularly true now, when he ended up giving a news conference on the steps of Capitol Hill in Washington DC, the heart of the American political arena.

His first port of call on his two-week trip to America was the United Nations headquarters in New York City. Here, after addressing world leaders yet again about debt relief at the Millennium Summit held on 7 September 2000, along with Nigerian President Olusegun Obasanjo, Bono presented to UN Secretary General Kofi Annan a petition containing 21.2 million signatures collected in over 150 countries. He impressed upon the journalists who jostled around him afterwards how vital it was to keep pushing this issue to the forefront.

Bono's determination to bend the ears of Congressmen and

women then propelled him straight to Washington, the seat of real power, where a kind of stalemate prevailed on the issue of debt relief.

The Clinton administration wanted Congress to sanction a payment of US$435 million, spread over a two-year period, which sum represented America's contribution to the Heavily Indebted Poor Countries Initative. Both the House of Representatives and the Senate were in favour of helping to ease the debt burden, but not necessarily to the tune of such a vast amount. Bono arrived in the capital to join the persuasion offensive, this involved attending a series of meetings with various political and church representatives.

Broadly speaking, Bono recognized the presence of abundant goodwill in Washington, but there was still the huge stumbling block of getting Congress to loosen the purse strings to the full amount. It was clear that he sometimes felt less than adequate to the task, when he openly stressed that it was really the place of people better qualified than himself to be doing this kind of horse trading.

Nevertheless, he waded in. In order to make a worthwhile contribution Bono knew that he needed the support and friendship of tough Washington political warriors, regardless of whether or not he agreed with their individual politics. On Wednesday, 20 September, he made one of these precious allies when he met with US Senator Jesse Helms, the chairman of the Senate Foreign Relations Committee, at his office in the Dirksen Senate office building.

The seventy-eight-year-old staunch Republican may have had to be helped up to speed by his Senate office staff on just who Bono was, in terms of his standing in the music world. And he had been too long in politics to be easily won over by a celebrity. But, by the conclusion of their meeting, Senator Helms had declared himself impressed by Bono's depth of character. More important, he had come round to the idea of cancelling the debt, even though his support was conditional at this stage.

The next morning Bono arrived on Capitol Hill at the House

Triangle where he met with individual Senators or their representatives. He was accompanied by US Treasury Secretary Lawrence Summers, White House Chief Economic Advisor Gene Sperling, House Budget Committee Chairman John Kasich and other Congressional supporters, including prominent Republican Senator Orrin Hatch.

At a televized news conference on the steps outside, Bono stood before a battery of cameras and fixed microphones in front of which dangled a poster with the bleakly uncompromising headline 'Today, 19,000 children will DIE'.

Beamed to a vast audience, Bono strenuously urged Congress to authorize the full payment of US$435 million. The universal will *was* there, he maintained, but sticklers for red tape were standing in the way. 'I'm asking,' he said directly to the small army of media before him, 'get your scissors and cut through the crap!'

It was blunt phraseology, Bono-style. Jamie Drummond reveals:

Bono's personal passion for the cause communicates absolutely to those with whom he meets face to face to discuss this issue. And he has an unusual strategy. In the past, on the whole, I would say that pop stars have got media coverage and they would say things to the media. But they have very rarely become such a finely tuned political lobbyist in the way that Bono has. And it has to be said that the person who put Bono on that track was actually Bob Geldof.

Bob was slightly wary of whether we would become a mass participation campaign. In the end, we did. But at one stage it wasn't necessarily the case that we were going to become one. And Bob suggested a kind of under-the-radar approach of just meeting with these politicians and trying to persuade them that they could make their names with this. And also to try to appeal to their humanity and to believe that these politicians have humanity, in a way that many campaigners traditionally have not and who have actually ended up alienating the very people whom they are trying to target.

Bono was always clear that that wasn't what he wanted to do. It was a bipartisan approach he favoured and that very much was what Jubilee 2000 was about, because it brought together the old left and the old right. We don't take those terms seriously anymore but Jubilee 2000 was certainly a place where everyone came together and Bono is at the very heart of it.

Of Bono personally, Jamie continues, 'He's got a good sense of humour. He's a bit scatty sometimes and he's extremely approachable. But he's a very unusual creature, because he can still be both a rock star and somehow a politician too.'

Having fulfilled his obligation to Jubilee 2000 for now, Bono had been due to return home anyway. However, his departure from America had been further hastened by yet another tragedy.

U2's new album would include a track dedicated to Bono's dead friend, INXS frontman Michael Hutchence. In the intervening years since 1997, Hutchence's heartbroken lover Paula Yates had been unable to come to terms with the singer's bizarre death.

She had suffered a nervous breakdown and depression had set in, which she had tried to alleviate through consumption of alcohol and drugs. She had made what was thought to be a suicide attempt, but had recovered, only to lurch into a decline that had systematically robbed the forty-year-old of her once pert rock chick looks and her zestful personality.

Her lonely despair had finally ended with a cocktail of drink and drugs that had left her dead, alone on her bed at her mews home in Notting Hill, West London, where, on the morning of Sunday, 17 September 2000, she was discovered by her four-year-old daughter by Hutchence. Heavenly Hiraani Tiger Lily, now orphaned, had tried in vain to shake her mum awake.

In response to the news, Bono and Ali had released a message of condolence through the press that read: 'Our first thoughts are for the four girls. It is their tragedy, more than anyone's. We know Bob [Geldof] is a great dad. They are a strong family but still our heart breaks.'

Bob Geldof indeed immediately took over the care of his former wife's and her lover's young daughter; the little girl could best be comforted by being with her older step-sisters. And the funeral service was arranged to take place in the church that was close to The Priory, the home that Paula and Bob had once shared in Davington, Kent.

Bono arrived back from America in time to join other mourners on Saturday, 23 September, at the funeral held in the twelfth-century St Mary Magdelene's church. Eighty people solemnly filed into the flower-filled church, among them a variety of stars from the worlds of television, film, music and fashion including Martin Kemp, Rupert Everett, Paul Young, Dave Stewart, Annie Lennox, Midge Ure, Jools Holland and Yasmin Le Bon. During the forty-five minute service, accompanied by Jools Holland at the piano, Bono sang the U2 number 'Bullet the Blue Sky'.

It must have been difficult to see blue skies in the immediate aftermath of this further waste of young life. And it would probably not have dulled the sadness any when the findings of the subsequent coroner's inquest pointed to the likelihood that Paula Yates had died accidentally from the mixture of booze and pills that she had taken, rather than having made a deliberate act to end her tormented life.

Life, however, went on, and in Bono's case U2 was about to release their first new record since 1998. This launch kicked off on 27 September when the band staged an open-air performance of two of their latest songs on the rooftop of the Clarence Hotel in Dublin.

As had happened thirteen years previously, when they had

brought bedlam to the streets of Los Angeles, this mid-afternoon mid-week performance brought hundreds of fans, at fairly short prior notice of the event, flocking to Dublin's city centre.

As if on cue, the sun broke through after the rain in time for the band to burst into life, playing two numbers, from the forthcoming album, called 'Beautiful Day' and 'Elevation'. Being 100 feet above ground level, Bono did not expect the band to be visible to the crowds massing on the pavements below, yet when he saluted the sea of people, the gesture produced a massive roar in response. Less happy were the police who were appearing in steadily growing numbers to control the crowd and to ensure the safe free flow of traffic while this stunt unfolded.

The setting saw Bono and the others standing on a variety of patterned rugs placed around the cold stone rooftop, in front of a giant TOTP (*Top of the Pops* logo) backdrop. The performance was to be broadcast on the long-running British music shown on Friday, 6 October.

Some fans became upset and critical when it turned out that during this rooftop performance that the band were not, in fact, performing live. For the sake of practicality, Bono instead sung each number over the top of a pre-recorded music and backing vocals track. But if there was any residual disgruntlement among U2 supporters, it did not harm sales. 'Beautiful Day' (for which the video had been filmed in August at the Charles de Gaulle airport in France) was released in Britain on 9 October 2000 and rocketed straight in at number one.

There were two CD single versions of the number. One version backed 'Beautiful Day' with two new tracks that would not feature on the upcoming new album, 'Summer Rain' and 'Always'. The other version paired the new A side with two live renditions of older numbers, 'Discotheque' and 'If You Wear That Velvet Dress'.

That 'Beautiful Day' was destined to top the charts instantly became obvious when in the first twenty-four hour period it sold 20,333 copies (nearly 9,000 copies more than the first day's sale of

11,527 notched up for 'Kids', a duet by pop superstar Robbie Williams and Kylie Minogue).

This fourth UK number one single for U2 meant much to Bono – even more than he had anticipated. He had certainly relished a return to making and performing music after what he described as having been too long part of the 'bowler hat and briefcase brigade'. Yet he had not realized how much U2 topping the pop charts would mean to him after all these years. It did not take him long to proclaim, 'It's great to be back.'

The focus tilted too towards the band's return to touring but all that was known as yet was that it would be likely to commence the following spring. To oil the wheels for this event, a series of low-key, select appearances had been arranged. The first of these took place on 19 October at the Man Ray Club in Paris when, before an intimate audience of 150, the band performed eight numbers, five of which came from the as-yet-unreleased new album. Four days later, in London, Bono and company played an exclusive live set for BBC Radio One from the Corporation's Maida Vale studios.

The single's chart-topping performance augured well for U2's new album release due in less than a week's time. In the three and a half years since the album *Pop*, the music scene had altered radically, with a huge upsurge in synthetically manufactured pop groups.

The days when a bunch of doggedly committed guys could hone their individual raw talents, before working the gruelling pub and club circuit, in order to fight their way to the Holy Grail of a recording contract, had long gone. Now would-be pop stars attended auditions held by music executives; and the prerequisites for passing such auditions seemed to be, not so much an ability to play instruments or to write original material, as good looks and the ability to dance. Frighteningly, image consultants and choreographers have become as crucial to success as record producers.

This was a trend that Bono now took the opportunity to lash out at. Declaring that the days of these acts were numbered, he announced, 'People are sick to the teeth of processed and hyped pop bands. It's crap!' He insisted that change was on its way, and that the music scene would soon see a return to real bands who actually played their instruments – bands like U2.

If there were those who viewed his words as evidence of arrogance, Bono had also clearly articulated the strong feelings of many, both inside and outside the music business, who are passionate about the value of real music. His brothers-in-arms on this front already included George Michael who had lambasted manufactured bands as being rubbish. And, more explicitly, Blur generalized current chart music as 'a load of shite'.

That U2 were still a real musical force to be reckoned with was confirmed when the new album, titled *All That You Can't Leave Behind*, released in Britain and Europe on 30 October, and a day later in America, seized the top slot both in the UK and in thirty-one other countries.

October 2000 marked twenty years since the release of U2's debut album *Boy* but although they were multi-millionaire rock stars now, none of the band were prepared to rest on their laurels. In content, the material embraced questions of mortality, suicide, sacrifice, terrorism, religion and personal crisis, and the band performed the songs using traditional stripped-down basic guitar, drums and bass.

They also treated it as if it were their very first album release, and threw everything into its promotion. Accordingly, U2 agreed to make their first actual studio performance in seventeen years for *Top of the Pops*; for this they were filmed performing three tracks at the show's studios at Elstree. A spokesperson for the show considered it a fantastic coup, and the first performance was broadcast on Friday, 3 November.

Critically, the album was well received, with the *Daily Mail* for one deciding that it captured 'U2 at their most spontaneous and direct'. Bono was direct enough when, in sending Prime Minister

Tony Blair a copy of the new album, he wrote on it the personal message, 'Don't let me down.'

In all likelihood this four-word exhortation referred to the British government implementing its pledge to cancel the proportion of Third World debt owed to the UK. It certainly coincided with President Bill Clinton signing a foreign aid bill on 6 November that provided the full US$435 million to enable the US to finance its share of the international Heavily Indebted Poor Countries Initiative.

Because of band commitments, Bono had not been free to attend the ceremony held in the East Room at the White House to mark this. But, in thanking all those who had lobbied hard for the bill, President Bill Clinton specifically praised the U2 frontman's fervent efforts on behalf of Jubilee 2000.

Band business had to take precedence right now, though, both at home and abroad. U2 now headed out around Europe, performing live in Madrid in mid-November as part of the Spanish Premios Amigo Awards. A week later they had crossed continents and by 23 November they were in Rio de Janeiro.

Whilst they were there, some Brazilian U2 fans gathered on the pavement outside the sumptuous hotel where the band was staying briefly got themselves into a lather fighting over a pair of black boxer shorts which had suddenly floated down from on high. Unsure whether or not the underwear actually came from a window on the floor occupied by the band, the fans still decided that the boxer shorts belonged to Bono and practically pulled them apart, squabbling over them.

The non-stop promo kept the band and the album sales buoyant, and news then emerged that U2 were to perform live at the Irving Plaza Club in New York City on 5 December.

One country which was unwilling to throw a welcoming arm around U2, however, was Burma. Bono – indeed the whole band – had been openly critical of Burma's military junta, outraged at the country's atrocious human rights record which included the practice of using forced labour, and of exercising a policy of ethnic cleansing against Shan, Karen and Karenni people, not to mention the existence of over 1,000 political prisoners in the country's jails.

As at November 2000, U2 were recommending that their fans should write to the British Foreign Secretary, Robin Cook, to urge that Britain refuse to participate in upcoming meetings with southeast Asian ministers, to be held in Laos in December, if the Burmese dictatorship continued to keep members of the National League for Democracy (NLD) under house arrest.

The NLD leader, Daw Aung San Suu Kyi, had been under house arrest since July 1989. The following year she had won a democratic election in Burma, but had been prevented from taking office because the military had staged a coup d'état that had established the dictatorship.

One ballad, 'Walk On', on *All That You Can't Leave Behind*, was dedicated to the dissident leader and that fact – together with the band's open criticism of the Burmese government – was enough for the authorities there to ban the album. Technically speaking, any person caught in possession of, or bringing or importing the album into Burma, could face a twenty-year jail sentence.

Safely on the other side of the world, Bono focused his attention on the latest in what was proving to be a successful string of warm-up dates, when U2 entertained a 1,000-strong audience at New York City's Irving Plaza Club. Celebrity fans in the audience that night included Hollywood superstar Tom Cruise, supermodel Cindy Crawford, actor Gabriel Byrne and the Corrs.

During the seventy-minute set of thirteen songs that spanned the band's career, the most poignant moment came when Bono dedicated a new number called 'Stuck in a Moment (You Can't Get Out Of)' to the late Michael Hutchence.

In the midst of thoughts of the death of friends – Hutchence and most recently Paula Yates – came also the promise of new life.

As ever, while Bono carried on with his career, Ali had continued to forge her own independent path and that involved championing particular projects.

Right then, she was still immersed in the Chernobyl Children's Project, which aims to provide medical aid for those children still affected by the fallout from the 1986 disaster. As Ali strove to ensure some quality of life for these victims, it was revealed that she was pregnant once more. With Elijah just sixteen months old, the Hewsons' fourth child would be due in June 2001.

All things being equal, Bono just might have finished the first leg of the new tour in time for the birth. On the back of the rip-roaring success of *All That You Can't Leave Behind*, it was a tour that was being wildly anticipated by U2 fans all over the globe.

After weeks of rumour and speculation, the official announcement finally came on 9 January 2001. Called 'Elevation', the world tour would commence on 24 March at the National Car Rental Center in Fort Lauderdale, Miami, where, due to demand, they had already had to add a second date scheduled for two days' later.

Thirty-three dates had originally been planned, spread over three months in North America and Canada. But before the tickets went on sale a further fifteen dates had to be accommodated. The extra gigs were at the Pengrowth Saddledome in Calgary; the San José Sports Arena, at Arrowhead Pond in Anaheim; the United Center, Chicago; the Palace of Auburn Hills in Detroit; Boston's Fleet Center; Philadelphia's First Union Center; and the MCI Center in Washington.

There was also going to be an extra date at Madison Square Garden in New York City and, three days later, an extra gig on 22 June at the Continental Airlines Arena in East Rutherford, New Jersey, which would end the American opening leg. For the first time since Zoo TV's opening stages in 1992, these gigs would all be played in indoor arenas.

The new year was barely a fortnight old and momentum was gathering. The single 'Beautiful Day' received three Grammy Award nominations for Song of the Year, Record of the Year and Best Rock Performance By a Duo or Group. *All That You Can't Leave Behind* had already sold in excess of six million copies and that figure was steadily rising. And a European tour, it was confirmed, would follow on from the US leg.

On 4 February 'Stuck In A Moment (You Can't Get Out Of)'/'Big Girls Are Best' went into the UK singles chart at number two. It was only now that Bono publicly revealed that 'Stuck In A Moment (You Can't Get Out Of)' was a tribute to Michael Hutchence. Originally, he had had no intention of letting this be widely known because, he said, Paula Yates had convinced herself that Hutch had not committed suicide. Because she had comforted herself with this belief – a belief that Bono now did not share – he had wanted to avoid perhaps offending her.

'Stuck In A Moment (You Can't Get Out Of)', Bono explained, addressed the guilt and anger associated with not being there (albeit unknowingly) for a friend who has nose-dived into a deep decline. Bono stated, 'In grief, anger is unexpected, but it's there.' He emphasised that the anger is directed inwardly at oneself.

There was scant time for introspection, however, for just two days later, at the annual NME Awards ceremony held at The Arches in East London, U2 overcame competition from AC/DC, the Beatles, Manic Street Preachers and Oasis, to walk off with the Best Rock Act trophy. This was a nice boost, with their upcoming tour now just six weeks away.

That night U2 also made off with a second prize – this time for the less than modestly named Godlike Genius Award. Within forty-eight hours one newspaper, the *Daily Record*, would question whether this latter accolade had temporarily gone to Bono's head.

Meanwhile, the day after the awards ceremony, on 7 February 2001, U2 played yet another warm-up gig, this time at the Astoria

Theatre in central London. It was billed as a return to their roots, a stripped-down show – much the same as would be proffered on the tour.

The show was an electrifying experience for the invited audience of 1,500, which comprised some lucky fan club members, a sizeable contingent from the music media and, of course, a fair smattering of celebrities who sat cheek by jowl, among them Mick Jagger, Jerry Hall, Bob Geldof, Salman Rushdie, Queen drummer Roger Taylor, DJ Chris Evans, the actor John Hurt, Kylie Minogue, Elvis Costello and teen sensation Billie Piper.

This was U2's first British show of this intimate size since they had played at London's Hammersmith Palais eighteen years before. During an urgent eighty-minute set, which began with 'Until the End of the World', went on to include 'Elevation', 'Stuck In A Moment (You Can't Get Out Of)', 'Discotheque', '11 o'Clock Tick Tock', 'Mysterious Ways' and 'One', and ended with '40' as the encore, the band lifted the rafters.

The enthusiasm of many in the audience led them to telephone friends, only to hold up their mobile phones to enable those on the other end to listen in on the gig. But it would have been hard to convey to those not actually there in person what was happening when the crowd reacted to a lean and energetic Bono, during the number 'Bad' near the end of the gig, leaping up to walk precariously along the top of a crowd rail whilst he sang. Bono, in fact, had used his own mobile phone earlier to serenade his pregnant wife Ali with the love song 'All I Want Is You'.

Generally speaking, the gig left U2 smelling of roses. What the *Daily Record* reported next day, though, was that, among the hundreds of fans gathered outside the venue, some were brandishing placards pleading for a ticket. One forlorn fan was quoted as commenting sadly that the gig had not, after all, been for the fans, but for the band itself.

The band, moreover, were reported to have arrived in a convoy of splendid identical Mercedes cars from which the four had stepped out, only to march straight inside the building, uncharacteristically without signing autographs.

The story's headline read 'Bono: "We're the best in the world!" U2 star's boast at intimate gig'. In fact, as became clear in the body of the article, what Bono had actually said was that U2 were applying for the job as best band in the world.

The honours, in any event, kept rolling in. On 9 February it emerged that Bono would, whilst in America on the Elevation Tour, give a commencement address on 6 June at Harvard University. At the same time he would also be made an honorary member of the graduating class of 2001.

In the midst of this welter of recognition though, Bono managed to remain focused when it came to those causes which he supported. The Los Angeles-based Conrad N. Hilton Foundation annually gives out the world's most lucrative humanitarian award to recognize those charitable bodies who diligently make an outstanding contribution to easing human misery around the world. In 2001, it emerged on 18 February, that Bono had written to the Foundation to nominate the Irish international relief organization Goal to receive this award.

It had been during his trip to Ethiopia during the 1980s famine disaster that Bono had first encountered the work of those in Goal and he knew that fifteen years later, aid workers from this relief agency were still out there.

One of Goal's founder members, John O'Shea, in response to the news that his organization had been nominated by the frontman told the *Belfast Telegraph*, 'It's especially pleasing to have been nominated by Bono because his commitment to humanitarian and environmental causes is well known worldwide.'

The next day U2 were en route to Los Angeles to attend rehearsals for the upcoming Grammy Awards. However, things got off on the wrong foot – as far as Bono was concerned – when the long haul flight on a British Airways plane screwed up his vocal cords.

There was no humidifier system installed on the aircraft and Bono blamed this for shredding his voice. A British Airways spokesperson later explained that, although the airline had previously tested the use of on-board humidifiers, they had not proved to make any appreciable difference to passenger comfort and so had been removed.

Still, Bono's fury at his dry throat spilled over at the sound check for the Grammys when he erupted angrily into a tirade. 'I'm sorry that my voice is so shite,' he is reported to have raged. 'But it's all down to British fucking Airways. I can only apologize to you.'

The 43rd Grammy Awards got underway on Wednesday, 21 February 2001, at the Staples Center. The annual ceremony was attracting more than its usual share of attention this year because of the presence of the Detroit-born singer Eminem, whose violent, homophobic lyrics were currently causing huge controversy on both sides of the Atlantic.

Gay superstar Elton John performed a duet with Eminem, but this did nothing to neutralize the outraged anger of the hundred-strong crowd of gay rights protesters who had gathered with placards to demonstrate against the rapper outside the building.

Inside the auditorium, Bono's earlier disappointment over the state of his voice was assuaged when U2 walked off with the trophy in each of the three categories in which the band had been nominated for 'Beautiful Day' – Record of the Year, Song of the Year and Best Rock Performance by a Duo or Group.

Accepting the coveted award for Record of the Year, Bono declared that U2 had not expected to win. He was, he said, experiencing a strange emotion. 'I think it's called humility,' he admitted, whilst holding aloft their latest prize.

Backstage at this event, in chirpy form, Bono joked about U2 being just another good-looking Irish boy band. But he was serious too when he explained that, although this three latest awards brought U2's haul of Grammys over the years up to ten, this time it was special. 'I don't remember really wanting it the way we wanted it tonight,' he said.

Having pulled off this hat trick, U2 flew out of America in the certain knowledge that the following week at the annual Brit Awards in London they were to be honoured with the Outstanding Contribution to Music prize, one of the industry's most prestigious awards.

Past winners include Queen, the Bee Gees, David Bowie and the Who; U2 were the first non British band to be given this special tribute. However, they were also nominated in the category of Best International Group, and for this prize they were in contention with legendary guitarist Carlos Santana, the Corrs, Savage Garden and Westlife.

Clearly, U2 were on a roll. The rehearsal for the Brit Awards had been so successful that it had turned into a two-hour impromptu gig for the private pleasure of the Earl's Court Arena technicians and staff.

The actual televized ceremony took place on 26 February. And, midway through the glittering evening, U2 filed on to the stage, having won the Best International Group award to receive their first trophy of the night from Australian singer Kylie Minogue and Huey Morgan from the band Fun Lovin' Criminals.

His fingers firmly wrapped around the distinctive slender statuette, Bono stooped towards the mike to say. 'This is the era of pop and of hip hop. We feel really great about the fact that this award is given to a guitar band with soul and with attitude. It's U2!'

The night's celebration of U2 continued as, before long, Elton John, there to present the Best International Male Solo award to Eminem, firstly took time out to declare, 'I want to thank U2 for all the great records over the years. They deserve all they get tonight.'

Traditionally, the Outstanding Contribution to Music category provides the endgame to the lengthy dazzling ceremony. U2's moment in the spotlight began with a giant video screen reminder of some of their finest moments to date, before the trophy was presented by Oasis songwriter Noel Gallagher who had wandered on stage to do the honours. Following his introductory speech, Gallagher charged the audience to 'be upstanding and show some respect for U2'.

After the clamour of applause died down, Edge was first to speak on behalf of the band. He said quietly, 'This is amazing. I want to thank the Brits for giving this award to an Irish band,' before going on to point out that in actual fact he had been born not in Ireland but in London, roughly 10 miles from where he now stood.

Taking over, Bono announced that other Brits deserving of U2's thanks included record producers Brian Eno and Steve Lillywhite, Island Records boss Chris Blackwell (whom Bono jokingly called 'a vampire'), the music publications *New Musical Express* and *Q*, as well as Radio One.

On a more personal note he wanted to express his deep appreciation to U2 fans for their loyalty through a variety of experimental phases in the band's long career. He said, 'Thanks very much for your patience. We've been in a few odd places over the years. Bless you.'

The show's two anchor presenters, television personalities Ant and Dec, declaring U2 to be the biggest band in the world, then left it to the four to stage the grand finale to the Brit Awards 2001 with a four-song medley of their hits, 'One', 'Beautiful Day', 'Until the End of the World' and 'Mysterious Ways'.

U2 turned in a blistering performance, invigorating the audience and easily living up to their latest accolade. The Outstanding Contribution to Music prize sometimes seems to denote the beginning of the end in a band's career. But, musically honed and brimful of confidence and authority, U2 were fairly bristling with power-packed energy.

Bono, dressed in his customary black, with designer stubble, was in magnificently magnetic form, imbuing the lyrics and his performance with barely contained passion. It was no surprise when ultimately, during the number 'Until the End of the World', the urge to get down among the crowd proved irresistible.

Despite repeated attempts by a security guy to steer the singer away, Bono, in full voice, strode among the throng of delighted people who slowly parted to let him through. Some men patted his shoulder or grasped his free hand as he passed, while occasionally a woman would steal a kiss or hook an arm around his neck for a hug.

Still evading capture by the now nervous security man, Bono climbed down through metal railings on to the floor of the auditorium to face the gleeful welcome of the crowd. Such was their enthusiasm at his near presence, that the singer was briefly hoisted aloft upon a few sturdy shoulders.

During the course of the evening Eminem had appeared on stage wearing a menacing white ice hockey mask and carrying a chainsaw for dramatic effect. And the usual profusion of female celebrities had braved the arctic February conditions in eye-popping scanty outfits for the barrage of photographers in attendance; model Caprice showed up wearing only a bikini, from which hung a curtain of beads. The event had overflowed with the exuberant delight of the stream of winners, and the tense undercurrent of the hidden deflation of the losers.

Although triple award-winner Robbie Williams was crowned the pop star who had won the most Brit Awards overall since their inception, many would agree that the night ended up belonging to U2. And the lasting image left with millions of television viewers was that of the glinting-eyed, unshaven Bono stalking towards, and singing up close into, the television camera, which coped with his unscripted intrusion by busily reversing along the rail track skirting the audience.

Backstage during the evening, whilst talking to the media, Bono took the time to pick up with Dominic Mohan, the *Sun*'s celebrity reporter, on a story he had read concerning himself in that newspaper two months earlier. The *Sun* had alleged that Bono had spent the evening in a restaurant openly flirting with the beautiful Irish singer Andrea Corr.

To straighten the record, Bono categorically dismissed any notion of romance between himself and Andrea Corr, who was literally just a good friend. His marriage to Ali, he was equally emphatic, was rock solid. Although far from being prone to sounding off about his private life, over the years Bono has repeatedly shown open admiration for his wife. And now he declared, 'She's a great woman.' After attending the post-gig party, Bono moved on to another shindig, before finally calling it a day around dawn.

On the face of it, for Bono, life in the recent past seemed to have been nothing but a whirl of back-slapping award ceremonies and boozy bashes. But, in fact, in the weekend between the Grammy Awards and the Brit Awards he had given a very different, private and sombre performance. Once more, it had been his sad task to sing at a friend's funeral – this time that of the French artist, Balthus, whose real name was Balthasar Klossowski, Count de Rola. Most noted for his erotic subject matter, the realist painter had held the distinction of being among a select few artists whose work was exhibited in Paris's Louvre art museum in their lifetime.

The funeral, attended by over 300 mourners, had been held on the Saturday at the local church in the Swiss village of Rossiniere. In the year 2000, U2 had performed at Balthus's ninety-second birthday party and it was as a family friend that Bono sang in tribute to the famous artist before he was interred at the place where there are plans to build a Balthus museum in his honour.

With the number of personal friends he had lost over the years, and because he so frequently confronted human suffering around the world through his involvement with various causes, Bono had never needed reminding of the presence of death in the midst of life. It meant that, regardless of showbiz razzmatazz, he was not inclined to forget where life's priorities really lay.

All the gratifying plaudits and the exciting tour preparations, therefore, did not stop him from diving headlong into yet another new cause – the Aids crisis facing South Africa. In early 2001, millions of people in that part of the world had already died of the incurable disease, with approximately another 4.7 million people already HIV infected. By 2005, it is estimated that average life expectantly in South Africa will have shrunk to thirty-eight.

Bono agreed with campaigners and humanitarian groups whose argument was with those giant pharmaceutical conglomerates who were refusing to supply anti-retroviral drugs cheaply, when the companies raked in billions of pounds annually. South African law had recently been changed in order to permit the purchase of generic drugs, thus keeping the pharmaceutical giants out of the picture. But thirty-nine drug manufacturers were taking issue with this, to the point of being prepared to go to court. It seemed immoral to Bono that, while the legalities were thrashed out, the death toll would inexorably rise.

A leading voice in this protest was, of course, Archbishop Desmond Tutu. He says:

A court case started in the first week of March but it was postponed because there was a body which wanted to be appointed as a friend of the court, so that it could join the South African government against the pharmaceuticals companies and the presiding judge allowed this to happen.

The pharmaceutical companies then said that they needed four months to be able to study the argument that this new body was presenting. The judge gave them a month-long postponement. Not four months. So a very interesting legal battle began.

The wonderful thing is, though, that so much of the world is, in fact, on the side of the victims. Because most of the people who have HIV Aids in Third World countries, so called, can't afford the very exorbitant prices that are being charged for medication. And many many people are dying, who need not die of this, if the drugs were more cheaply available.

We have seen in Europe and in the United States that to be diagnosed with Aids is no longer the death sentence that it used to be a few years ago. I mean, they are almost ghoulish, these pharmaceutical giants, to insist so much on profit. You see, they don't want generic drugs to be made available which are cheaper than the brand name drugs.

It was no surprise to Archbishop Tutu that Bono would choose to throw himself into this cause too. Bono acknowledged that he felt even more intensely concerned about world health issues as his own family grew in size. And he saw no reason not to liken the plague-like Aids epidemic to other manmade atrocities that had been responsible for wiping out hundreds of thousands of human beings, such as Hiroshima and Auschwitz. His mission is to mobilize the political will needed to reduce the cost of drugs to allow people the chance to begin to tackle this scourge. And he vowed to use whatever clout he has, to that end.

Jamie Drummond confirms:

The HIV crisis in South Africa sees 11,000 people infected every day and 5,500 people die each day. These are awfully grim statistics and we think that the world's richest nations can both afford to do more and *have* to do more. Not just for moral reasons. But in terms of their own enlightened self-interest. You can't see Africa grow sick and die like this and although certain Africans are fighting to stop it, they need assistance.

We work closely with African leaders and Bono is very keen to put together a package which is, in the short term, more debt cancellation. And, in the longer term, a kind of holistic package of initiatives to make sure that Africans can take care of themselves.

The situation took a dramatic turn in late April when the giant drug manufacturers unexpectedly dropped their legal action. It had been a public relations disaster for the pharmaceutical companies involved and campaigners were jubilant at the climb-down. But, more importantly, this most welcome development offered the South African government an opportunity to give hope to the country's millions of Aids and HIV sufferers.

Bono's other debt cancellation work for Third World countries, of course, also continues. Jamie Drummond says, 'Jubilee 2000 has been reincarnated as Drop the Debt and Bono is still banging on doors. He is at the forefront now of trying to force President George W. Bush and US Secretary of State Colin Powell to push for further debt cancellation.'

His touring commitments had never stopped Bono from helping the various causes with which he was involved and this new issue in South Africa just added to the list. Meanwhile, the band continued rehearsals at Hanover Studios in Dublin – rehearsals that had started earlier in the month, in readiness for the upcoming tour.

In March, those rehearsals switched to Miami, and further details were now emerging. P. J. Harvey would be the opening act throughout the tour, the theme of which would be travel and luggage.

Of the intended, ruthlessly stripped-down, return-to-basics style, Edge said, 'We started out in clubs and want to get back into how it used to be.' And all four welcomed the focus being placed on the music and its delivery, rather than on a feast of visual stage props.

On 6 March then the European dates were officially announced. This leg would be taking in sixteen major cities, commencing on 6 July in Denmark. Wending its way around the continent, visiting Sweden, Germany, France, Switzerland and Spain, among other countries, the tour would then enter its latter stages, coming to Britain for an 11 August date at the *Manchester Evening News* Arena.

Three days later, U2 were promised at the National Exhibition Centre in Birmingham. After which, to the dismay of the band's Scottish fans, without playing a single gig north of the border, U2 would head to London for an Earl's Court concert on 18 February.

Precisely one week later, on 25 August 2001, the final gig of the Elevation Tour would take place at Slane Castle, near Dublin. This gig would be the band's first concert in Ireland since 1997. It would also mark the twentieth anniversary of their last live appearance at the castle, when they had played support there to Thin Lizzy in 1981.

The European tour official announcement also let it be known that this final gig was intended to be a ten-hour event, with support bands Coldplay, the Red Hot Chili Peppers, Kelis, JJ72 and Relish in attendance.

Following their recent award ceremony appearances, the huge upsurge in interest in U2 had resulted in all of their albums re-charting, with *All That You Can't Leave Behind* – five months after its release – zooming back up to number three in the British album charts.

Now, further proof that U2 was literally the hottest ticket in town was provided on 10 March 2001 when the tickets specifically for the Slane Castle gig went on sale and there was a frenzied stampede. All 80,000 tickets sold out in just over half an hour.

Although this was breathtakingly impressive, it also meant that many fans (hundreds of whom had queued outdoors for twenty-four hours) were left frustrated and upset at missing out. Angry scenes were reported at some Dublin ticket outlets and the existing police presence had to be reinforced, with one arrest being made.

Sensitive to the strength of the fans' feelings, the next day Bono and the band tried to arrange an additional Slane Castle gig. But this proved to be a harder undertaking than anyone imagined.

It transpired that to organize a second Slane Castle gig would require local authority planning permission. Bono appealed to the Minister for the Environment to find a way around this snag, but a spokesman for the minister replied that he could not do so.

Bono promptly put out an appeal to the Irish Prime Minister, Bertie Ahern, to intervene instead. Bono told the press, 'As far as we are concerned, what looks to be a disaster at the moment, could become one of the greatest days ever.' Whether his optimism would prove to be well-founded would remain to be seen.

By mid-March U2 could not put a foot wrong. At the Meteor Ireland Music Awards, staged at Dublin's Point Theatre, on St Patrick's Day, the band won the Best Irish Band award, and the Best Album award for *All That You Can't Leave Behind*. Bono and Edge also jointly won the Best Songwriter award.

The glitzy award ceremony in Dublin was attended by, among other stars, Elton John, Ronan Keating, Sinead O'Connor and Christy Moore. U2, of course, could not be there in person and they accepted their latest clutch of trophies by video link to the United States. Bono thanked the audience back home with the words, 'We love that you gave us this award for our album because we love our album. And love is in the air!'

By now the Elevation Tour was among the year's most anticipated musical events, even though tickets for some of the American gigs were priced at US$120 (£93). At the last moment there had had to be a change of support act when rock singer P. J. Harvey was reluctantly forced to pull out of appearing at the first four gigs because of a reported bout of glandular fever. She intended joining U2's tour in early April instead, but in the meantime the Corrs were asked to fill the opening night vacancy. Andrea Corr declared, 'We're all thrilled. We couldn't believe it!'

Opening night itself on Saturday, 24 March, at the National Car Rental Center in Fort Lauderdale, was hailed as being sensational. As promised, the stage setting was almost bare, free of flashy gimmicks, and all the more effective because of it.

A definite theme had emerged. A week earlier Bono had declared, 'Love is in the air!' The outline of a heart had appeared depicted inside a piece of x-rayed luggage that formed part of *All That You Can't Leave Behind*'s video images. And now, strikingly, the stage extended outward, deep into the crowd with two gigantic parallel and generously curved gangways which met at a point to form a heart shape.

Opening with the number 'Elevation', Bono and the band burned their way through a scintillating set that was crammed with classic U2 songs to complement the now familiar new material. And all the way Bono threw himself passionately into the perform-ance. When he was not reaching out into the crowd, almost being pulled off his feet by grasping hands, he was hurtling around every square inch of the unusually shaped stage.

Touts had exchanged tickets for upwards of £1,000 outside, prior to the gig. For two hours inside the arena, the band electrified the 20,000 fans, proving that they had no need, after all, of osten-tatious stage props, special effects or sophisticated gadgetry to enthrall an audience. And the cutest trick of the night was that, somehow, U2 managed to make a packed arena feel as intimate as a downtown nightclub. The success of this opening night provided U2 with all the confidence they required for the months ahead.

Crisscrossing the states, U2 blasted their way across America. Whether they were in Georgia, Oregeon, Illinois or New York state, they not only proved that they were back with a vengeance, but also that they had the right to reclaim the title of biggest band in the world.

In mid-April, well into their stride, U2 took time out during their sold-out appearance at San Diego's Sports Arena to pay public tribute to Joey Ramone, of the 1970s punk rock band the Ramones. Joey had recently died and that night U2 dedicated their perform-ance of three numbers to the late frontman.

Days later, it was revealed that the already award-laden 'Beautiful Day' had been nominated for yet another prize, this time in the Best Contemporary Song category in the upcoming annual Ivor Novello Awards.

It also emerged around now that Bono had reportedly purchased a plush sixteenth-floor apartment in an exclusive building, popular with celebrities, which overlooks New York's Central Park.

U2 had tried to organize their concert dates to accommodate the arrival of Bono and Ali's fourth child, but in the event the singer had to make an unscheduled dash home to Ireland from the US to be with his wife, who on 20 May 2001 gave birth at a Dublin hospital to another baby boy. Now with a family of two sons and two daughters, a thrilled Bono joked, 'And I'm only half Catholic. I feel really blessed.'

He and his family would not be occupying this new home until at least June and, anyway, at this point, Bono had to remain entirely focused on the tour. Months before, the singer had warned that he viewed climbing back on to the rock stage as akin to stepping up to a title fight – losing was not part of the plan.

But U2 did not lose. The Elevation Tour consolidated the chart-topping global triumph of *All That Your Can't Leave Behind* – an album that *Rolling Stone* had now decided was U2's third masterpiece, after *The Joshua Tree* and *Achtung Baby*. By thoroughly thrilling their worldwide legion of fans, they have captivated a whole new generation of devotees along the way.

Bono's natural dynamism propelled him into producing many memorable performances which, in addition to bringing him personal satisfaction, further established his right to take his place alongside Mick Jagger and Freddie Mercury as one of *the* three all-time top frontmen in rock music.

Bono, of course, has always been more than a rock star. A distinctive and fascinating figure, he is as much at home on stage as he is prowling the corridors of power, meeting with, and earning the respect of, world political and religious leaders.

Admittedly, Bono is not the only rock star with a strong social conscience. But political activism and a tireless commitment to good causes have been constant features of his career, during which he has steadfastly maintained the courage of his convictions irrespective of whether he is praised or ridiculed for them.

A hugely persuasive man, he can be charismatic and mischievous as well as suffocatingly intense. Once he has the bit between his teeth he does not let go, and there is a disconcerting bald honesty about him that has seduced music-lovers worldwide and penetrated the hardened defences of seasoned politicians.

For stretches of his life he has run the risk of near canonization because of his crusading zeal and also because his strong morals make him uninterested in the vacuous hedonism indulged in by many of his music contemporaries. Uncomfortable with even the notion of such a saintly mantle, yet it is true that his spiritual faith has always been a solace to him.

U2 have currently sold in excess of 100 million albums worldwide. But Bono has no patience with living on past glories. Forever forward-looking, like his bandmates, he will continue to musically push the envelope as far as it will go. Likewise, he will continue to crave vast improvements in a world that – even with his unbridled optimism – he describes as being still an unfair and often wicked place.

Fame, fortune and respect from others for what he has so far helped to achieve is not enough for him. 'I am not in any way at peace,' he recently declared. 'I'll always be a bit restless.'

His many facets reflect his many contradictions, and his willingness to expose his own vulnerabilities merely seems to illuminate his strengths. He is a genuine pacifist, yet he is capable of a militant attitude, and he carries within himself an inner, insoluble rage.

And it is this central duality, right at the core of Bono's personality, that ultimately intrigues. Indeed, it ensures that in an overcrowded and competitive industry, where idols have their transient place in the sun, Bono is, and will always remain, unique.

Discography

Singles

FIRE
Released **8 August 1981**
Highest chart position 35

GLORIA
Released **17 October 1981**
Highest chart position 55

A CELEBRATION
Released **3 April 1982**
Highest chart position 47

NEW YEAR'S DAY
Released **22 January 1983**
Highest chart position 10

TWO HEARTS BEAT AS ONE
Released **2 April 1983**
Highest chart position 18

PRIDE (IN THE NAME OF LOVE)
Released **15 September 1984**
Highest chart position 3

THE UNFORGETTABLE FIRE
Released **4 May 1985**
Highest chart position 6

WITH OR WITHOUT YOU
Released **28 March 1987**
Highest chart position 4

**I STILL HAVEN'T FOUND WHAT
I'M LOOKING FOR**
Released **6 June 1987**
Highest chart position 6

**WHERE THE STREETS HAVE NO
NAME**
Released **12 September 1987**
Highest chart position 4

IN GOD'S COUNTRY
Released **26 December 1987**
Highest chart position 48

DESIRE
Released **1 October 1988**
Highest chart position 1

ANGEL OF HARLEM
Released **17 December 1988**
Highest chart position 9

WHEN LOVE COMES TO TOWN
Released **15 April 1989**
Highest chart position 6

ALL I WANT IS YOU
Released 24 June 1989
Highest chart position 4

THE FLY
Released 2 November 1991
Highest chart position 1

MYSTERIOUS WAYS
Released 4 January 1992
Highest chart position 13

ONE
Released 7 March 1992
Highest chart position 7

EVEN BETTER THAN THE REAL
    THING
Released 20 June 1992
Highest chart position 12

WHO'S GONNA RIDE YOUR WILD
    HORSES
Released 5 December 1992
Highest chart position 14

STAY (FARAWAY, SO CLOSE)
Released 4 December 1993
Highest chart position 4

HOLD ME, THRILL ME, KISS ME,
    KILL ME
Released 17 June 1995
Highest chart position 2

DISCOTHEQUE
Released 15 February 1997
Highest chart position 1

LAST NIGHT ON EARTH
Released 2 August 1997
Highest chart position 10

PLEASE
Released 4 October 1997
Highest chart position 7

IF GOD WILL SEND HIS ANGELS
Released 20 December 1997
Highest chart position 12

SWEETEST THING
Released 31 October 1998
Highest chart position 3

BEAUTIFUL DAY
Released 9 October 2000
Highest chart position 1

STUCK IN A MOMENT (YOU
    CAN'T GET OUT OF)
Released 4 February 2001
Highest chart position 2

Albums

BOY
Released October 1980
Highest chart position 52

OCTOBER
Released 24 October 1981
Highest chart position 11

WAR
Released 12 March 1983
Highest chart position 1

U2 LIVE UNDER A BLOOD RED
SKY
Released 3 December 1983
Highest chart position 2

THE UNFORGETTABLE FIRE
Released 13 October 1984
Highest chart position 1

WIDE AWAKE IN AMERICA
Released 27 July 1985
Highest chart position 11

THE JOSHUA TREE
Released 21 March 1987
Highest chart position 1

RATTLE AND HUM
Released 22 October 1988
Highest chart position 1

ACHTUNG BABY
Released 30 November 1991
Highest chart position 2

ZOOROPA
Released 17 July 1993
Highest chart position 1

POP
Released 15 March 1997
Highest chart position 1

ALL THAT YOU CAN'T LEAVE
BEHIND
Released 31 October 2000
Highest chart position 1

Index